Pacific Bounty

Hawaii Cooks with
Roy Yamaguchi

With Marty Wentzel

As seen on Public Television and underwritten by
Mauna Loa Macadamia Nut Corporation

KQED, Inc.
San Francisco

KQED Books and Tapes
2601 Mariposa Street
San Francisco, CA 94110

Publisher: *Pamela Byers*

Project Editor: *David Gancher*

Writer: *Marty Wentzel*

Book Design: *Amaryllis Design and Kajun Graphics*

Food Photography: *Rae Huo, RJH Photography*

Food Styling: *Nina Schneider*

Cover Design: *Sharon Smith Design*

Cover and Interior Illustrations: *Karen Barbour*

Printed by Penn&Ink in Hong Kong

For KQED:

President & CEO: *Mary G.F. Bitterman*

Vice President for Publishing & New Ventures: *Mark K. Powelson*

Library of Congress Cataloging-in-Publication Data

Yamaguchi, Roy, 1956–
    Pacific bounty : Hawaii cooks with Roy Yamaguchi / Roy Yamaguchi with Marty Wentzel.
        p.   cm.
    Includes index.
    ISBN 0-912333-23-5 (pbk.) : $16.95
    1. Cookery, Hawaiian. I. Wentzel, Marty. II. Title.
TX724.5.H3Y28   1994
641.59969--dc20   94-17391
                                                                                 CIP
                                                                                 Rev.

10 9 8 7 6 5 4 3 2 1

Distributed to the trade by Publishers Group West

Contents

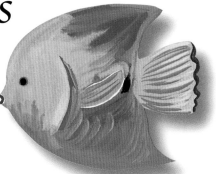

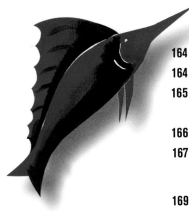

Foreword

The production of Hawaii Cooks with Roy Yamaguchi, *the television series, and* Pacific Bounty: Hawaii Cooks with Roy Yamaguchi, *the book, was a concerted effort by many people. It would take far too much space to acknowledge everyone associated with the various facets of the television series, but I especially want to thank:*

Melanie Kosaka, executive producer and creator of Hawaii Cooks, *for providing the opportunity to showcase Hawaii's distinctive foods and rich culture; Robert Bates, supervising producer, for his ability to merge the creative and technical aspects of television; Chuck Furuya, master sommelier, and Robert Kowal, wine segment producer, for their knowledge of and inspiration on wine; Grace Akazawa for designing the* Hawaii Cooks *logo; Chris Conybeare for his legal advice and vast knowledge of public television; the production staff of Hawaii Public Television, for their patience and constant support; the chefs who generously shared their time and recipes; and the Mauna Loa Macadamia Nut Corporation, the Hawaii State Department of Agriculture, Castle & Cooke Properties, and the Department of Business, Economic Development and Tourism, the series underwriters, whose generous support makes* Hawaii Cooks *possible.*

For their help with the development and production of the cookbook, I am grateful to: Marty Wentzel, my coauthor, whose imagination and attention to detail was essential to creating the menus, the recipes, and the vision behind them; Mark Powelson, KQED's vice president for publishing, for seeing the national potential in what started off as a local series; Pamela Byers, publisher of KQED Books, whose vision of publishing excellence was so abundantly realized; David Gancher, project manager, who pulled together and shaped the many pieces of the project; Marianne Ackerman, Pat Koren and Laurie Smith, whose art direction and production so fully captured the spirit of the work in design; Rae Huo, food photographer, and Nina Pfaffenbach Schneider, food stylist, for their imaginative and precise handling of the food photography; Sharon Smith, cover designer, and Karen Barbour, the cover artist, whose work captured the playful and bold spirit of Pacific Bounty.

Introduction

A culinary revolution has taken root in Hawaii.

We are a growing legion of chefs who go out of our way to get the plumpest ahi (yellowfin tuna) at the Honolulu fish auction. We get dirt under our fingernails in order to taste sweet upcountry Maui strawberries. We milk floppy-eared Nubian goats on the Big Island to learn how rich Puna goat cheese is made. We monitor the availability of crops from one end of the archipelago to the other, and we urge growers to cultivate new products with us in mind.

The result of our efforts is a fresh new cuisine. My colleagues and I are passionately committed to ingredients that have been grown on Hawaii's soil or caught in waters off its shores, and we have been able to translate them into dishes such as green bean salad with Maui onions and Kau oranges; grilled Lanai venison salad; stirfry of wild mushrooms with Puna goat cheese; and cassoulet of Kahuku shrimp in a lemongrass-basil broth.

Our theory is simple: Diners in Hawaii should be able to taste Hawaii. Why eat a flavorless tomato that has been mass-produced, gassed and shipped from the mainland, when you can have a juicy, vine-ripened tomato from the Big Island? Why eat a fillet of sole frozen two months ago, when you can have a delicate grilled shutome (Hawaii swordfish) caught this morning? In its purest form, Hawaii cuisine provides the palate with the sweetness of our sun, the saltiness of our surf and the richness of our land.

We are not afraid to import international ingredients such as Greek olives, Italian parmesan and French truffles. But to create true Hawaii cuisine, we must turn to the products of Hawaii whenever possible, whether it is Kona yearling beef from Palani Ranch or salad greens from a farmer on Molokai. The growers and fishermen give us a beautiful, flavorful product, and we, in turn, help them build their businesses.

Our islands have long been ripe for a new cuisine. Through the 1970s and most of the 1980s, Hawaii's menus generally offered foods such as Norwegian salmon, Maine lobster and midwestern beef. Separated from the mainland by thousands of miles, island chefs were forced to settle for ingredients that were canned, frozen, packaged or half-ripened.

The hotel-building boom of the 1980s brought a new wave of chefs to Hawaii, many to work in the visitor industry, others to start their own restaurants. These young chefs began to seek out food sources in their own backyard. Small-restaurant owners began to talk with farmers; chefs in some of the larger hotels took notice and followed suit, encouraging their staffs to work primarily with Hawaii produce, fish and livestock.

In the early 1990s, chefs started talking about these trends. We opened our address books and shared phone numbers of specialty farms that we had discovered, and our movement gained momentum. We toured neighboring island farms to learn more about their operations, and we networked with growers to keep informed about what they produce.

Our cause has been furthered by Hawaii's exceptional growing conditions. Rich volcanic soil combined with perennial warmth, sunny skies and ample rains give rise to luscious fruits, such as bananas, papayas, pineapples, poha (cape gooseberries), ohelo (similar to the cranberry), coconuts, guava, mangoes, lilikoi (passion fruit), oranges, limes and kumquats.

Chefs on every island now have year-round access to the freshest of vegetables: Japanese eggplant, ulu (breadfruit), pohole ferns (related to the fiddlehead), mixed baby greens and vine-ripened tomatoes, as well as more island-specific products such as purple Molokai sweet potatoes and sweet Maui onions.

We are equally blessed with remarkably fresh seafood: mahimahi (dolphinfish), opaka-paka (pink snapper), shutome (swordfish) and moana (goatfish), to name a few. Our long list of local shellfish includes sweet shrimp, lobster and the prized opihi (limpet). Aquacultural efforts on the North Shore of Oahu and the west side of the Big Island produce California abalone, Maine lobster and a half-dozen types of edible limu (seaweed). Locally grown herbs and seasonings such as ginger root, garlic, chilis and lemongrass allow us to experiment with distinctive Asian flavors.

In addition, we have discovered the benefits of working with flavorful local livestock, such as Big Island beef and lamb, and Lanai venison. We have enjoyed further culinary flexibility by calling on Hawaii's own processed products, such as Big Island-produced macadamia nuts, Kona coffee and Hawaii chocolate.

Hawaii flavors are elusive and evolving. We are not slaves to European or Asian techniques. We are creating a cuisine at once insular and international, combining natural local ingredients with cultural influences from around the world.

It only makes sense that we should have a cuisine of many cultures, for Hawaii itself is defined by a population of immigrants. More than 1,000 years ago, the earliest Hawaiians grew fish in man-made shoreline ponds, planted taro (a nutritious tuber) and cooked pigs in imu (underground ovens). In the mid to late 19th century, Chinese and Japanese sugar plantation workers brought, respectively, wok cooking and exquisite preparations of raw fish. Over the decades they were followed by Portuguese, Koreans, Filipinos, Mexicans, Vietnamese and other ethnic groups, each of whom contributed unique culinary styles to their new home.

To define Hawaii's new cuisine even further, one must consider the personalities and backgrounds of our chefs. Philippe Padovani, from France, is equally at home making a Hawaiian-style mignonette by adding ogo (seaweed), ginger and mirin (sweet Japanese wine) as he is creating a Mediterranean tabbouleh with wok-fried moana. Texas-born Amy Ferguson-Ota cures a wild boar loin with sesame seeds, lemongrass and ginger, then serves it with a guava sauce.

Sam Choy pays tribute to his native Hawaii with dishes like Kahuku prawns with a Japanese soba (buckwheat) noodle salad. And, while I was raised in Japan and often visited my grandparents on Maui, I also enjoy working with techniques from Italy and China.

For all of our cultural differences, we are united in our common goal: to establish Hawaii as a place for outstanding dining. It is a philosophy that has encouraged the use of not only Hawaii products, but distinctive foods of every region around the world.

I encourage you to translate our vision into one of your own. Substitute ingredients that grow near you. Purchase fish that has been caught locally, livestock from your closest ranches and fruits and vegetables from farmers' markets. Seek out ingredients from ethnic markets. Above all, share these recipes with family and friends in the true spirit of aloha.

The Chefs

Roy Yamaguchi

Many people say that Roy Yamaguchi is Hawaii's best-known chef. He adheres to the home-grown philosophy of Hawaii cuisine, yet he has also crafted a distinctive culinary style out of which has grown worldwide fame and recognition; in 1993, for instance, the James Beard Foundation named him the best chef in the Pacific and Northwest.

Yamaguchi calls his style Euro-Asian in honor of his training in classical French and Italian cooking, his Japanese upbringing and his frequent visits with his grandparents on Maui.

Yamaguchi's early proficiency at cooking home-fried Portuguese sausage and eggs eventually led him to study at the Culinary Institute of America in New York. After a quick rise through apprenticeships at L'Escoffier and Michael's and a stint as executive chef at Le Serene, he got his big break at one of Los Angeles' most prestigious restaurants, L'Ermitage, where he worked closely with legendary chefs Jean Bertranou and Michel Blanchet.

Eager to create his own style, Yamaguchi opened 385 North in 1984. Here was a restaurant where Hollywood's elite mingled over such ambitious experiments as ginger shrimp pot stickers in roasted bell pepper sauce, and spicy mussels with crispy noodles in Szechuan black bean sauce. Despite his rising L.A. profile, however, Yamaguchi longed to open a smaller, more personal restaurant in Hawaii, where he saw the most potential for his East-meets-West bent. In 1988, he launched the flagship Roy's in the Oahu suburb of Hawaii Kai, followed by two ventures on Maui, Roy's Kahana Bar and Grill and Nicolina's.

Chef Yamaguchi has since opened restaurants in the Guam Hilton and Roy's Tokyo in Setagaya-ku and he is currently in the process of opening Roy's Poipu Bar and Grill on Kauai. His heart, however, remains in the kitchen. "Working in the kitchen is what I love most," he says.

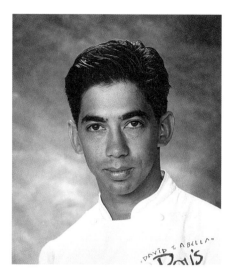

David Abella

David Abella enters his kitchen with an open mind. "I look around to see what's fresh and available to work with," he explains. "I think about textures, colors and shapes of ingredients, and how I can make them different. I try to taste a dish before I've made it." From there, the real test of his food is whether or not it's good enough to serve to a family member. "I put my heart into each plate and give it my best."

From age 17 on, Abella worked as a busboy and chef, but he never considered a restaurant as anything more than a job—until he met Roy Yamaguchi, that is. In 1989, Abella landed a position at Roy's in Hawaii Kai, where he worked his way from line cook to sous chef. "Roy is the toughest, fairest boss I've ever had," says Abella. "He totally changed my attitude about cooking and showed me how to work with finesse. His palate is so sophisticated; even after five years of collaborating, I still can't come close to his expertise."

In early 1992, Yamaguchi had enough faith in his protégé to ask him to head the kitchen at the new Roy's on Maui. There, Abella has remained true to his mentor's Euro-Asian style while developing a reputation for his own inventions, such as imu-roasted pork with lilikoi (passion fruit) apple sauce.

Honolulu born and bred, Abella has a soft spot for Hawaii's no-frills "local" foods: plate lunches with "two scoop rice" and teriyaki beef; chili and rice; and manapua and pork hash (types of dim sum). But his Chinese and haole (Caucasian) heritage and his daily contact with the islands' many cultures are more evident in his present-day menus. Consider his hibachi-grilled salmon, which has a teriyaki sauce and fresh Asian vegetables; and his crispy hamachi (yellowtail) rolls, which come with a decidedly Eastern sauce of Japanese plum sake and Chinese chilis.

Sam Choy
Kona Hilton
Executive Chef

Sam Choy

Sam Choy looks every bit the part of the successful chef. His ample girth suggests a vast yet intimate knowledge of food, and his broad smile brightens up the room like a fluorescent aloha shirt.

Choy talks about his childhood on Oahu's North Shore with characteristic sentiment: "When I was in elementary school, my father catered weekly luau for up to 800 guests at a time. I couldn't wait for the weekend so that I could help him with soaking the long rice, cutting the green onions and skinning the salmon for the lomilomi. And man, how I loved the smoky smell of those 250-pound pigs when they were pulled from the imu (underground oven)."

Choy ventured beyond his roots for 18 months to work as an executive sous chef at New York's Waldorf Astoria Hotel. "Coming from friendly Hawaii, it was a shock looking at the massive number of people moving around New York City with no smiling faces. It woke me up a bit. But I'm the kind of person who fits in anywhere, and pretty soon I was making friends, going to ball games and having a good time." Choy introduced Waldorf diners to tropical tastes such as lilikoi (passion fruit) glazes and macadamia nut breast of chicken, and he came away with his eyes wide open to the potential of the food industry.

Back home, Choy came into his own as executive chef of the Kona Hilton, and today he runs two Big Island diner-style restaurants bearing his name. The formica tables are generally jammed with fishermen, construction workers and tourists who have been clued in on the quality of Choy's menu. He taps his Hawaiian-Chinese heritage with foods like an updated version of the traditional luau dish called laulau (ti leaves wrapped around steamed fish) with fresh vegetables. And he swears allegiance to the foods he grew up with, like barbecued ribs with teriyaki sauce, or honey duck with sauce made from oranges grown in the Big Island region of Kau. Of late, Choy can be spotted traveling across Europe, Asia and the U.S. to promote the Hawaii stylings for which he stands.

Kathleen Daelemans

When Kathleen Daelemans describes her childhood in Florida, she summons up the smells of her father's homemade bread, visits to ethnic markets and perpetual motion in the kitchen. "My whole family is artistic, and we all love to eat," she says. "Plus, my grandmother and her five sisters grew up in Naples, so it followed that I would end up expressing myself through cooking." Starting as a counter girl, dishwasher and chef's assistant at Yosemite's Ahwahnee Hotel, her career finally took off during her three-year apprenticeship with chef Judy Rogers at San Francisco's Zuni Cafe. "Judy taught me the integrity of ingredients," recalls Daelemans. "She showed me just how crucial it is to develop close relationships with farmers."

In 1991, Daelemans signed on with Maui's Grand Wailea Resort & Spa as chef of its Cafe Kula. There, she quickly tuned into the Hawaii cuisine mind-set, making friends with growers who were willing to experiment with new crops for the resort. In particular she found a kindred spirit in farmer Robbie Friedlander, who, by 10:30 each morning, has delivered the day's organic harvest—Maui corn, apple bananas, snap peas—to her doorstep.

Standing five-foot-two, Daelemans weighed 195 pounds when she designed the cafe's menus, and during the next two years, she lost 65 pounds by eating her own food. Her dishes are high in fiber and low in fat, which means she replaces bacon and fried eggs with turkey hash and frittatas, and she sautés chicken in a reduction of stock and garlic puree rather than oil or butter.

On the sunny piazza which defines the cafe, diners follow Daelemans' credo of "moderate, don't eliminate." Big plates are loaded with black bean salad spiced with cilantro, Vietnamese chili paste and balsamic vinegar, served in a ripe papaya. Hawaii is a natural for such healthy cuisine thanks to its abundance of fresh foods, but Daelemans adds that in any part of the world, "a food that is low in fat, sodium and cholesterol can still have great flavor."

Amy Ferguson-Ota

Amy Ferguson-Ota is not easily pigeonholed. She was born in Texas, but her culinary touchstones range from her Creole grandmother's jambalaya to beurre blanc classes at Le Cordon Bleu in Paris. In her dishes such as sesame-cured boar loin with guava dressing, and lilikoi (passion fruit) sorbet, food specialists have been known to detect Southwestern, French and Hawaiian influences, but Ferguson-Ota calls it as she sees it. "I believe in being regional," she says. "Ever since I was a girl, I've loved visiting the farmers' markets. My favorites were the watermelon stands where they'd cut you big, icy slices, and you'd sit at a picnic table just slurping it up."

Ferguson-Ota strengthened her personal commitment to local products as executive chef of the Hotel Hana-Maui. It was an easy transition, since many of the raw ingredients found in her native Texas—papayas, chili peppers, avocados—are abundant in the islands. Neighbors stopped looking twice when she rushed off at dawn to pick fresh pohole (a long, tender fern) for a salad, and long-time Maui residents taught her how to wrap fish in ti leaves for steaming, a dish she still serves today. "When I think of Hawaiian cooking, the preparation is what counts," she says, "the salting, preserving, drying and pickling." She has learned even more from her Hawaii-born husband, whom she calls a "master of the old cooking techniques. He cooks a pig in an imu (underground oven) exactly the way the old Hawaiians did."

Today, as executive chef of the Ritz-Carlton Mauna Lani on the Big Island, the busy Ferguson-Ota sends her sous chef out to pick the pohole, but she continues to make a point of talking with farmers, fishermen and aquaculture producers several times a week. And on the weekends, if she sees an ulu (breadfruit) tree on the side of the road, she doesn't think twice about pulling over, climbing on the roof of her car and picking some for the evening's vichyssoise.

Chuck Furuya

Chuck Furuya belies the image of the sophisticated oenophile. "All too often you see stone-faced people sitting around in black tie discussing things like fermentation," he says, "but I'm an easy-going guy. One of the greatest experiences I ever had was pairing wines with hamburgers."

Furuya was born in Colorado, where his father, a Hawaii native, was stationed in the Armed Forces. After formative years in Europe and the Orient, he settled in Hawaii to attend college and work restaurant jobs. By "being in the right place at the right time," he steadily developed his natural knack for wine selection, which landed him sommelier posts at such prestigious Honolulu dining rooms as Maile in the Kahala Hilton and the former Bagwell's 2424. Today, he consults for Fine Wine Imports, judges international wine events and conducts restaurant staff training and public tastings around the state.

Most notably, Furuya is a Master Sommelier, a member of the prestigious guild of international wine experts based in England; there are only 23 Americans in the guild and 39 active members overall. "When you become a Master Sommelier, people think it's like winning the Olympic gold medal," he says. "They assume you're one of the tops in the field. To me, passing the Master Sommelier exam was more of a personal goal. By no means do I feel that I'm better than the next person at tasting. Wine is far too subjective for that."

These days, Furuya is savoring the new challenge of matching wines with Hawaii cuisine. "The new cuisine is so dynamic and bold—and something you can't get anywhere else in the world—so it's very exciting for me to work with it," he says. For this book, he recommends many vintages of a slightly fruity nature to help offset the spiciness of Hawaii cuisine; for instance, a chenin blanc from the Loire Valley paired with hot Thai-style roasted shutome (sword-fish), or a refreshing German Riesling with zesty Asian spring rolls. "In Hawaii's warm climate, you don't want a cumbersome wine; you want something cool, something that wakes you up."

Beverly Gannon

"I haven't found any place I'd rather be than Maui," says Beverly Gannon, gazing out the window of her Makawao home at a view of pineapple fields, west Maui mountains and a wide swath of sea. "Even better, in two minutes I can be at the restaurant." She is referring to Haliimaile General Store, the 1925 plantation camp store that she and her husband, Joe, transformed into a restaurant in 1988 after her five-year-old catering business outgrew their house.

Located 1,200 feet up the slopes of Mt. Haleakala, in Maui's most prolific farm country, Haliimaile General Store is just a short drive away from a cadre of growers who bring Gannon newly picked vine-ripened tomatoes and other fresh vegetables on short notice. "Hawaii has started listening to the people who are taking things out of the ground to put on the plate," she says. "I'm really happy with the agricultural network here."

Such dedication to freshness had nothing to do with her childhood, however. "Everything we ate came out of a can or a freezer, and it was always overcooked," she says in a soft drawl reflecting her Dallas roots. "My mother always used head lettuce, and she would cook a fillet of fish for an hour." Not until she reached her 20s, when she worked as road manager for Liza Minnelli and Joey Heatherton from 1978 to 1983, did Gannon discover just how good food can taste. "In the entertainment business, I was around people who were always being wined and dined. I realized that fish could taste pretty good when it was cooked right!"

Her eyes opened to the potential of cooking, Gannon moved to London to study at the Cordon Bleu cooking school. "My most important lesson was to just get in there and do it. There's nothing to be afraid of in the kitchen. Ninety percent of the time, if you use the best ingredients, it's pretty hard to go wrong." Today, at her well-received restaurant with its bright front dining room and softly lit back room decorated with local artwork, Gannon's signature dishes demonstrate a no-holds-barred approach to Hawaii cuisine, from sashimi tartare with Japanese caviar and shiso (beefsteak) leaf, to grilled ahi (tuna) with tomato, starfruit and an orange beurre blanc.

Jean-Marie Josselin

Jean-Marie Josselin once wanted to be a butcher—until he came face-to-face with the slaughterhouse, that is. "They make you carry 200-pound slabs of meat," says the Frenchman. "I realized that I'm just not cut out for it." Instead he sought the more palatable profession of chef, first mastering the basics at the Culinary School of Paris, then making a name for himself with menus for the Rosewood chain's luxurious Crescent Court Hotel in Dallas.

When Josselin moved to Hawaii to become chef of the Hotel Hana-Maui, his professional and personal perspectives took a radical about-face. He made friends with fishermen, who taught him the best places to catch mahimahi and shrimp. He stopped by backyard barbecues, where he learned how to roast huli-huli chicken over a fire made of guava and mango wood and banana and ti leaves. He met people of many ethnicities, who shared with him such age-old recipes as Portuguese bean soup and Chinese stirfry. And he met Sophie, his Maui-born wife and business partner, creator of the colorful plates for his dining rooms.

Such heartfelt island experiences seasoned Josselin's classical concepts with Hawaiian accents and helped him create a cuisine that he describes as "fresh local foods imbued with Asian, European and Californian techniques." At his Maui and Kauai restaurants, both called A Pacific Cafe, his broad-minded sensibilities are embodied in dishes such as seared opakapaka (pink snapper) with black Thai risotto in a red curry coconut sauce, and Peking duck and shrimp tacos with papaya-ginger salsa.

In a way, Josselin has come full circle from his formative years, when he lived on his grandparents' farm in Burgundy. As a boy, he learned how to appreciate the richness of newly harvested mushrooms and the sweetness of strawberries straight out of the garden. Today, on his own farm in Kilauea on Kauai, he grows 95 percent of the produce used at A Pacific Cafe.

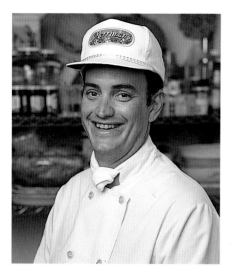

Peter Merriman

Peter Merriman scored a hit with his fellow Boy Scouts when he made eggs Benedict over an open fire. In high school, his football teammates were equally impressed when he whipped up salade Niçoise at parties. Today, in his namesake restaurant in the Big Island ranch town of Waimea, this respected chef continues to take the boyish approach to entertaining, from wearing a baseball cap as part of his uniform to stepping out of the kitchen to joke with his diners.

Merriman's earliest culinary fires were stoked by his mother, a food writer. She introduced her son to dozens of famous chefs, and by age 16 he was ready to follow their lead. His first real restaurant job was doing "grunt work"—peeling carrots, making coffee, playing gofer— for Ferdinand Metz, who now heads the Culinary Institute of America. "He is a truly inspirational man," says Merriman. "His spirit of cooking is something that I still carry with me."

When Merriman moved to the Big Island to work at Mauna Lani Resort's Gallery restaurant, he was immediately disenchanted with the quality of the canned beans and imported tomatoes used by most chefs at the time. He started going outside the conventional food sources, tapping home-grown products instead, and by the time he opened Merriman's in 1988, he had earned his current reputation as friend to dozens of island farmers, fishermen and ranchers.

Considered by many to be the founder of the Hawaii Regional Cuisine organization, Merriman first assembled a dozen chefs in 1991 simply to "talk-story" (a Hawaiian-style rap session). Instead, the group became responsible for the growth of an impressive communication network between local chefs and growers all over the Hawaiian Islands. Merriman is so dedicated to the cause that it's not uncommon to find him holding a meeting in a cattle pasture or conferring in a strawberry patch. He shows off local ingredients to their fullest in dishes such as wok-charred ahi, free-range Waimea veal in mango-peppercorn sauce and taro-chili cakes, but he nonchalantly shrugs off fame by placing the spotlight on the food producers: "They're the ones who make me look really smart."

Sergio Mitrotti

Sergio Mitrotti has always exhibited an adventurous spirit, first as an avid sailor and scuba diver in the Mediterranean, then as a successful graphic artist in his native Italy, then as the proprietor of a high-end clothing store in Beverly Hills.

But for this Renaissance man, food has always been the most natural of all avenues for exploration. "In Italy, you eat well from the moment you're born," he says. "When I was a teenager, I didn't think twice about making gourmet food for parties." The decision to cook professionally came in 1987, hand in hand with the desire to leave Los Angeles and its fast pace and move to Hawaii, which he saw as the perfect place to pursue his many passions. "I was ready to open a restaurant," he says. "I was an amateur cook, but a sophisticated eater."

Mitrotti's lack of formal culinary training didn't faze Honolulu diners. They embraced his Cafe Cambio in 1988, followed in 1991 by Cafe Sistina, a trendy restaurant known for its late-night live jazz and linguine alla puttanesca. The walls of Cafe Sistina double as Mitrotti's canvas; he is painting a replica of part of the Sistine Chapel on the wall behind the bar. "Cooking is very much like art. I try a little of this and a little of that, and as long as I can experiment, I'm happy."

This culinary Marco Polo has brought to Hawaii a strong whiff of authentic Italian cooking, as in his spinach ravioli with gorgonzola or his gnocchi with lamb sausage, and he continues to explore new worlds with his version of Spanish paella and Middle Eastern couscous. In the past five years, his food has taken on decidedly Hawaiian overtones, as he adds a Japanese shiso (beefsteak) leaf to a plate of scallops and bay shrimp, or buys local macadamia nuts for his petti di pollo, or brings in basil from a windward Oahu grower for pesto butter. "Being Mediterranean, I have found an environment in Hawaii that's natural to me," he says. "I feel very much at home here."

Philippe Padovani

Philippe Padovani took the long route from his native France to Hawaii: via Australia. At age eight he accompanied his adventurous parents to the outback, where they opened a small snack shop called the Moulin Rouge. "For Australia in the 1960s, it was quite progressive," says Padovani. "Farmers from hundreds of miles away would stop to eat there." When he wasn't playing with his pet wallaby or studying animal tracks, he worked in the Moulin Rouge's kitchen, flipping hamburgers and cooking up chicken rolls, steaks and fish. By the time his family returned to France the 14-year-old Philippe "knew the reality of what food was about; I was hooked."

From a prestigious post as head of the kitchen at Restaurant La Tour Rose in Lyon, France, to high-profile positions in Hawaii, Padovani learned to adjust his cooking to wherever he was in the world. "You have to have a feeling about cooking. Making a recipe is one thing, but helping it reach its peak point of flavor requires a special touch." In 1992, as the new executive chef of Lanai's Manele Bay Hotel, he acted on that philosophy by developing a specific style of cooking for the tiny island, much of which is based on the daily knock at the kitchen door. Sometimes it's a local fisherman peering into the kitchen, displaying a gargantuan tuna caught just two hours before. Other days it's a farmer holding a paper bag, offering papaya and pineapple he picked that morning. As Padovani sees it, "the local farmers and fishermen are the heart and soul of Lanai cuisine."

Padovani injects his Lanai flavors with a decidedly French flair. His dishes range from fresh salmon smoked with aromatic island wood, to opakapaka and onaga (both snappers) steamed in ti leaves. He is a major devotee of Hawaiian Vintage Chocolate, a brand of chocolate made from Big Island cocoa beans, and he shows it off to its best advantage in his exotic fresh fruits with chocolate lilikoi (passion fruit) sabayon.

Darin Schulz

Darin Schulz sees his profession as one long, continuing education program; for instance, he still remembers the Michigan dishwasher who showed him how to pit cherries with a paper clip. During his seven years in Hawaii, Schulz furthered his schooling by absorbing all he could in the Asian kitchen. "I'll never forget standing in the Ritz-Carlton Mauna Lani and watching a Japanese cook make miso (fermented soy paste) soup," he says. "He did it by second nature, but it was all new to me."

As executive chef of Lanai's Lodge at Koele from 1991 to 1993, Schulz drew from the sources of the island to fashion dishes such as roasted Lanai venison with lilikoi (passion fruit) marinade. He encouraged community farmers to grow produce to the hotel's specifications, and soon he had access to five different kinds of vine-ripened tomatoes, beets, zucchini blossoms and baby green beans. "It was great for all of us. It helped the farmers make a profit, and helped me learn about local products like Japanese eggplant and ong choy (Chinese water spinach)."

Of course, cooking with home-grown foods was nothing new to Schulz. In the backyard of his boyhood home in Colorado grew a garden so prolific that he and his siblings would load up their wagons with the excess corn, asparagus, strawberries and squash and sell them door-to-door. "My dad had four kids for a reason," he laughs. "Working in the garden was an essential one-hour portion of our daily chores."

East Meets West in Hawaii

While Hawaii delivers the familiarity of an American state, more than 60 percent of its residents can trace their roots to Asia and the Pacific; still others hail from mainland America, Europe and points east. In Honolulu alone, the cultural mix is astounding. A Japanese department store sells kimono and futon, while next door, its mainland-style counterpart displays nightgowns and bedroom furniture. In downtown Honolulu, restaurants and nightclubs of every description rub elbows. Friends of Mediterranean ancestry link arms for raucous line dances at an annual Greek Festival in Ala Moana Beach Park.

Hawaii cuisine is equally polyethnic, as it blends the flavors, textures and cooking styles of Hawaii, Asia and Europe. Menus around the state invite dreams of world travel, with their Japanese hamachi (yellowtail) rolls, Italian linguine, Thai spring rolls, Vietnamese pho (noodle soup with hearty garnishes), Chinese dim sum, Korean kim chee, Mexican tacos, Indian curries, German wienerschnitzel and Portugese chorizo (sausage).

Cassoulet of Kahuku Shrimp in a Lemongrass Basil Broth

Mixed Plate

Roy Yamaguchi

Chicken Spring Roll with Cucumber Mango Relish

Roasted Shiitake Salad with a Ginger Tomato Vinaigrette

Cassoulet of Kahuku Shrimp in a Lemongrass Basil Broth

Warm Papaya Tart

APPETIZER
Chicken Spring Roll with Cucumber Mango Relish

Available in Asian markets, rice paper is a thin, round sheet made of ground rice and salt. Use the standard 8-inch size in the following recipe. Makes 10 spring rolls.

Chicken Mixture
½ teaspoon minced ginger
¼ teaspoon minced basil
½ teaspoon minced garlic
1 teaspoon minced lemongrass
¼ cup chopped green onion
2 tablespoons olive oil
¼ cup dried shiitake mushrooms
¼ cup dried water chestnuts
¼ cup bean thread noodles, boiled, strained and coarsely chopped
¼ cup finely chopped mustard cabbage (Chinese cabbage) or Napa cabbage
1½ teaspoons fish sauce
1 pound raw chicken, coarsely chopped

Preparation of the Chicken Mixture
■ In a skillet, brown the ginger, basil, garlic, lemongrass and green onion in the oil over high heat for 10 seconds.
■ Add the mushrooms, water chestnuts, noodles and mustard cabbage and sauté for 1 minute.
■ Season the mixture with the fish sauce, and place it in a large bowl. Once it has cooled, add the chicken and mix all ingredients well.
■ Season the mixture with more fish sauce or salt and pepper if needed.

Preparation of the Spring Rolls
■ Dissolve the sugar in the hot water. Dip each rice paper wrapper in the sugar water until it is flexible.

Spring Rolls

1 teaspoon sugar
1 cup hot water
10 (8-inch) rice paper wrappers
1 quart frying oil

Relish

1 tablespoon minced ginger
1/4 teaspoon minced garlic
2 tablespoons olive oil
1/2 teaspoon spicy sesame oil
1/2 cup seedless cucumber, diced, skin on
1/2 cup tomatoes, diced
1/2 cup mango, diced
1/4 teaspoon soy sauce
1 teaspoon Lingham chili sauce, or any
　　spicy/sweet sauce

- Place 1/2 cup of the chicken mixture near the bottom edge of each piece of rice paper. Fold both edges in and continue to roll.
- Deep-fry the rolls in the oil at 375 degrees for 15 minutes, or until they turn golden brown.

Preparation of the Relish

- Sauté the ginger and garlic in the olive oil and sesame oil in a small pan over medium heat for about 10 seconds.
- Quickly add the cucumber, tomato and mango. Toss the mixture for 10 seconds.
- Remove the mixture from the heat and season it with soy sauce and chili sauce.

Assembly

- Cut the spring rolls in half. Place the slices on the plate, cut side down, and garnish with the relish.

SALAD

Roasted Shiitake Salad with a Ginger Tomato Vinaigrette

Chef Yamaguchi pairs the earthy flavor of shiitake mushrooms with a tangy, Asian-inspired vinaigrette. Serves 4.

Mushrooms

28 fresh shiitake mushroom caps, or button
　　mushroom caps
Salt to taste
1 tablespoon cracked peppercorns
4 tablespoons olive oil

Preparation of the Mushrooms

- Preheat the oven to 350 degrees F.
- Place the mushroom caps on a sheet pan. Sprinkle them with the salt and cracked pepper. Coat them with olive oil and roast in the oven for about 15 minutes or until soft.

Preparation of the Salad Mixture

- Sauté the eggplant in the oil over high heat for about 30 seconds.

31

Salad Mixture

¼ cup julienned Japanese eggplant, skin on
   (2 inch length)
2 tablespoons olive oil
Salt and pepper to taste
4½ cups mizuna, romaine or your favorite lettuce
2 artichoke bottoms, julienned
20 basil leaves, whole
¼ cup bean sprouts
3 cups radicchio, or red cabbage

Vinaigrette

1 teaspoon minced garlic
1 teaspoon minced shallots
1 teaspoon minced ginger
3 tablespoons olive oil
3 tablespoons sesame oil
2½ tablespoons rice wine vinegar, or any delicate
   vinegar
½ tomato peeled, seeded and minced
1 cup fresh basil, julienned
3 tablespoons soy sauce

Season with the salt and pepper. In a large bowl combine the eggplant with the mizuna, artichoke bottoms, basil leaves, bean sprouts and radicchio. Set aside.

Preparation of the Vinaigrette

■ Sauté the garlic, shallots and ginger in the olive oil and sesame oil over moderate heat for 10 seconds, until they turn golden brown.

■ Add the vinegar, tomatoes, basil and soy sauce and cook for 15 seconds.

■ Remove the vinaigrette from the heat and pour it over the salad mixture. Mix well.

Assembly

■ Divide the salad mixture evenly among 4 plates. On each plate, place 7 shiitake mushrooms around the lettuce.

ENTREE

Cassoulet of Kahuku Shrimp in a Lemongrass Basil Broth

Hawaii cuisine at its best: fresh local shrimp paired with a traditional French butter sauce and Thai-style seasonings. Serves 4.

White Butter Sauce

¼ cup dry white wine (chablis or
   chardonnay)
1 tablespoon white vinegar
1 shallot, chopped
¼ cup heavy cream
2 cups unsalted butter
Salt and white pepper to taste

Preparation of the White Butter Sauce (makes 2 cups)

■ Simmer the wine, vinegar and shallots in a medium saucepan over low heat. Reduce the mixture 10 to 20 minutes, to 1 teaspoon. (Note: The wine, vinegar and shallot reduction will last for 1 week when covered and refrigerated.)

■ Add the cream and reduce by ⅓, for 1 minute, to 3 tablespoons. Add the butter slowly and whisk the mixture.

■ Add the salt and pepper to taste. Strain the sauce and keep it warm in a double boiler at 120 degrees for no longer than 4 hours.

Cassoulet

60 whole Kahuku shrimp (1 pound contains 30-40 shrimp), or regular frozen (16-20 size) shrimp
Salt and pepper to taste
2 tablespoons olive oil
¼ cup julienned red bell pepper
1 teaspoon minced lemongrass stalk
1 teaspoon minced ginger
¼ cup julienned yellow bell pepper
¼ cup diced onions
¼ cup diced tomatoes
¼ cup diced celery
1 teaspoon minced garlic
2 cups fresh shiitake mushrooms, sliced
1 teaspoon minced cilantro
1 cup julienned basil
8 ounces raw scallops, diced
⅛ teaspoon hichimi (a Japanese spice blend), or to taste

Garnish

24 broccoli florets
1 sheet nori (dried seaweed), cut into ⅛- by 2-inch strips (optional)

Preparation of the Cassoulet

- Peel the shells off the shrimp, leaving the heads and tails on.
- Salt and pepper the shrimp.
- Heat the olive oil in a large skillet. Add the red bell pepper, lemongrass, ginger, yellow bell pepper, onions, tomatoes, celery and garlic. Sauté the mixture for 30 seconds.
- Add the mushrooms, cilantro, basil and scallops, and sauté for 30 seconds.
- Add the shrimp and cook the mixture until the shrimp are medium in doneness. Add the hichimi, then stir in 1 cup of the white butter sauce.

Assembly

- Serve the cassoulet in 4 soup bowls. Garnish it with broccoli florets and nori strips (optional).

Wine Suggestion

Zilliken, Estate Riesling, Saar, Germany, *or*
Nautilus, Sauvignon Blanc, Hawkes Bay, New Zealand

Warm Papaya Tart

This dessert can also be made as a pear or peach tart. Serves 8 to 10.

Dough

2 cups pastry flour
2 sticks plus 3 tablespoons butter
¼ cup plus 1½ tablespoons granulated sugar
1 egg yolk

Filling

3 eggs
1 cup sugar
1 tablespoon all-purpose flour
1½ sticks unsalted butter
1 cup chopped papaya
½ cup roasted Hawaiian macadamia nuts

Preparation of the Dough

■ Preheat the oven to 350 degrees F.
■ Place all the ingredients in a food processor, and blend for 1 minute, until they form a ball.
■ Remove the dough, and refrigerate for 30 minutes.
■ Roll the dough to ⅛-inch thickness. Place it in a 12-inch tart shell and bake it for 45 minutes. Remove the shell from the oven and let it cool.

Preparation of the Filling

■ Cream the eggs, sugar and flour in a medium bowl.
■ Brown the butter in a sauté pan for 1½ minutes, until it has a nutty flavor. Add the butter to the egg/sugar/flour mixture.
■ Gently fold in the papaya and nuts.

Assembly

■ Preheat the oven to 350 degrees F.
■ Turn the mixture into the tart shell and bake it for 40 minutes.

The Local Gourmet

Sam Choy

Baked Brie with Macadamia Nuts

Tahitian Crabmeat Soup

Kahuku Prawns "Fried Poke" Style with Soba Noodle Salad

Burnt Cream with Kona Coffee

A P P E T I Z E R
Baked Brie with Macadamia Nuts

Native to Australia, macadamias were first planted in Hawaii in 1892. Today, thousands of acres of the trees thrive in the tropics, particularly on the Big Island where Chef Choy is based. Serves 4.

Ingredients
2 (4½ ounce) rounds of brie cheese
1 tablespoon flour
1 large egg, lightly beaten
½ cup finely chopped Hawaiian macadamia nuts
½ cup panko (Japanese shaved bread crumbs) or
   any unseasoned fresh bread crumbs
Poha preserves or mango chutney
Lavosh and thinly sliced apple for
   accompaniments

Assembly
■ Cut the brie in half or leave it whole. Coat the brie with the flour.
■ Dip the coated brie in the egg.
■ In a shallow dish, combine the macadamia nuts and panko. Coat the brie well on all sides with the macadamia nut mixture, patting the mixture on to help it adhere.
■ Chill the brie for 30 minutes.
■ Preheat the oven to 400 degrees F.
■ Bake the brie for 10 minutes or until the crust is golden brown.
■ Transfer the brie carefully to a platter and serve it hot with poha preserves, lavosh (thin, crunchy bread sprinkled with sesame seeds) and apple slices.

Tahitian Crabmeat Soup

This rich South Pacific-inspired soup goes well with warm, fresh-baked bread. Serves 8.

Ingredients

2 cups diced onion
¼ cup butter
2 tablespoons flour
2 cups heavy cream
1½ cups chicken stock
2 cups coconut milk
2 cups frozen chopped spinach, thawed, or 3 cups chopped fresh spinach, washed and stemmed
1½ cups lump crabmeat
Salt and white pepper to taste

Assembly

■ In a large saucepan, sauté the onions in the butter until they are translucent. Stir in the flour and blend the ingredients well.
■ Add the heavy cream and chicken stock, and simmer for 5 minutes, stirring frequently.
■ Stir in the coconut milk, spinach and crabmeat and cook for 3 minutes, stirring frequently.
■ Season the soup to taste with the salt and pepper.

Kahuku Prawns "Fried Poke" Style with Soba Noodle Salad

Soba is the Japanese name for buckwheat noodles, a thin pasta with a robust flavor. Here, Sam Choy tops his soba with a fried version of poke, the popular Hawaiian pupu (appetizer) made of bite-size pieces of marinated fish. Serves 4.

Poke Mixture

½ cup soy sauce
1 tablespoon olive oil
1 tablespoon sesame oil
1 tablespoon finely sliced peeled ginger
1 tablespoon minced garlic
24 whole raw prawns, medium-size
1 cup chopped fresh seaweed
1 cup sliced won bok cabbage

Preparation of the Poke Mixture

■ Mix the soy sauce, olive oil, sesame oil, ginger and garlic in a large bowl. Marinate the prawns (shell on), seaweed and won bok in the mixture for 30 minutes.

Kahuku Prawns "Fried Poke" Style with Soba Noodle Salad

Soba Salad

1 tablespoon soy sauce
1 tablespoon sesame oil
Salt and pepper to taste
16 ounces cooked Japanese soba (buckwheat)
  noodles
½ cup diced red peppers
½ cup diced yellow peppers
½ cup sliced snow peas
½ cup sugar snap peas
½ cup chopped carrots
Cilantro to taste

Vinaigrette

¼ cup olive oil
3 tangerines, sliced in half
2 tablespoons soy sauce
1 tablespoon brown sugar
1 tablespoon sesame oil
½ teaspoon grated ginger

Salad Greens

1 pound mixed baby greens

Ingredients

2 cups heavy cream
6 eggs
½ cup sugar
6 tablespoons brown sugar
½ tablespoon freeze-dried Kona coffee
2 teaspoons vanilla
6 teaspoons sugar for topping

Preparation of the Soba Salad

- Mix the soy sauce, sesame oil, salt and pepper in a medium bowl. Toss the soba and vegetables in the mixture. Sprinkle in the cilantro, toss the mixture lightly and set it aside.

Preparation of the Vinaigrette

- Heat the olive oil in a medium pan. Add the poke mixture to the pan, and cook it over medium heat for 5 minutes, or until the prawns are fully cooked.
- Remove the poke mixture from the pan and set it aside, leaving the liquid in the pan. Over low heat, squeeze the tangerine juice into pan. Add the soy sauce, brown sugar, sesame oil and ginger.
- Blend all the ingredients, and keep them warm.

Assembly

- On a plate, place the soba salad over the salad greens. Next, artfully arrange the cooked poke mixture over the soba salad, and top it with the warm vinaigrette.

DESSERT

Burnt Cream with Kona Coffee

Named for the southwestern region of the Big Island where it thrives, Kona coffee ranks as one of the world's best-quality beans. Serves 6.

Assembly

- Preheat the oven to 350 degrees F.
- In a heavy saucepan, heat the cream over low heat until bubbles form around the edges.
- In a medium mixing bowl, combine the eggs, sugar, brown sugar and coffee, and whisk the ingredients until they are slightly thick.
- Gradually whisk the heavy cream into the egg mixture. Stir in the vanilla.

- Pour the mixture into six (6-ounce) custard cups. Place the cups in a baking pan and pour hot water halfway up the outside of the cups.
- Bake the mixture for 45 minutes, or until it has set.
- Refrigerate the burnt cream until it is well chilled.
- Sprinkle each cup with 1 teaspoon of sugar. Place the cups under the broiler and cook the burnt cream until the topping is bubbly.
- Chill until serving time.

Wine Suggestion
Ca'del Solo, Malvasia Bianca, California

Noodles

Asia boasts a centuries-old tradition of making noodles from rice, soybean, buckwheat and vegetable starches. Italy has long been considered the world capital of pasta, which is generally made of wheat but sometimes spinach and potatoes as well. This spectrum of starches—and their preparations—finds common ground in Hawaii, where linguine primavera (Italian pasta with fresh vegetables) is as easy to come by as beef lo mein (with Chinese wheat noodles), pad Thai (with stirfried rice noodles) and Japanese soba (with buckwheat noodles).

Certain Hawaii restaurants make their own noodles; others purchase them from a 50-year-old family enterprise called Crown Noodles. Each year, Crown turns out tons of pastas for Chinese, Vietnamese, Japanese, Filipino and Italian menus, along with products unique to Hawaii—most notably, a luau pasta made from the leaves of the taro plant.

When gathering ingredients for the oriental noodle dishes throughout this cookbook, seek out the Asian markets in your area. For Italian recipes, check the gourmet section of your grocery store; in addition, Italian restaurants sometimes sell homemade linguine, fettuccine and spaghetti. Happily, cross-cultural substitutions are generally acceptable in Italian and Asian recipes. Angel hair pasta can take the place of bean thread noodles, for instance, and linguine can be substituted for rice noodles.

Petti Di Pollo Alla Macadamia (Chicken with Pasta, Sun-Dried Tomatoes and Macadamia Paste)

Flavors of the Mediterranean

Sergio Mitrotti

Frittata Di Zucchini (Baked Zucchini Omelette)

Insalata Italiano (Italian Salad with Peppers, Tomatoes, Capers and Olives)

Petti Di Pollo Alla Macadamia (Chicken with Pasta, Sun-Dried Tomatoes and
  Macadamia Paste)

Lattaiolo (Italian Custard)

APPETIZER

Frittata Di Zucchini (Baked Zucchini Omelette)

Italy's answer to the quiche, this dish is best when served hot. Serves 6.

Ingredients

¼ cup extra-virgin olive oil
1½ pounds zucchini, thinly sliced
1 medium onion, thinly sliced
4 eggs
Salt and pepper to taste
¼ cup flour
½ cup grated parmesan cheese
¼ cup chopped parsley

Assembly

■ Preheat the oven to 350 degrees F.
■ Heat the olive oil in a medium pan. Sauté the zucchini and onion in the oil. Stir until all the liquids are released by the zucchini, and evaporate the liquids. Cook the mixture until it is golden brown.
■ Whisk the eggs, salt, pepper, flour and parmesan in a large bowl; then add the zucchini and onion mixture. Mix well.
■ Pour the mixture into a greased 10-inch skillet or baking pan. Bake the frittata for 45 minutes, until it is golden brown.
■ Slice the frittata into small pieces, and garnish it with the parsley.

Insalata Italiano (Italian Salad with Peppers, Tomatoes, Capers and Olives)

If Kalamata olives—or pickled Greek olives—are not available, Chef Mitrotti suggests using black California olives in this peasant-style salad. Serves 6.

Pepper and Onion Mixture
2 red bell peppers, julienned
1 onion, julienned
¼ cup olive oil

Italian Dressing
2 tablespoons chopped garlic
½ teaspoon black pepper
½ teaspoon salt
½ cup balsamic vinegar
½ cup olive oil

Salad
1 head radicchio
1 head romaine lettuce
2 tomatoes, chopped
¼ cup capers
½ cup chopped Kalamata olives, or black olives
2 cups pepperoncini peppers

Preparation of the Pepper and Onion Mixture
- Sauté the bell pepper and onions in the oil over medium heat for 2 minutes, or until they are less than fully cooked; they should remain firm.
- Cool the mixture to room temperature.

Preparation of the Italian Dressing
- Place all the ingredients in a bowl, and stir until mixed.

Assembly
- Break the radicchio and romaine into a large serving bowl.
- Sprinkle the pepper and onion mixture, tomatoes, capers and olives over the lettuce.
- Gently squeeze the juice from the pepperoncini peppers over the salad, then sprinkle the peppers over the salad.
- Sprinkle 1/2 cup of the Italian dressing over the salad.

Petti Di Pollo Alla Macadamia (Chicken with Pasta, Sun-Dried Tomatoes and Macadamia Paste)

Hawaiian macadamia nuts add a rich and exotic flavor to a Mediterranean classic. Serves 4.

Pasta
12 ounces dried penne or mostaccioli pasta

Macadamia Paste
1 cup diced Hawaiian macadamia nuts, roasted
¼ cup olive oil

Chicken and Sauce
1 pound boneless chicken breasts, diced and
   lightly floured
½ tablespoon extra-virgin olive oil
Salt and black pepper to taste
1 tablespoon minced garlic
1 pound mushrooms, sliced
¼ cup sliced sun-dried tomatoes
½ cup whole basil leaves
1 shot brandy
1 cup half-and-half
¼ cup grated parmesan cheese

Garnish
2 tablespoons diced Hawaiian macadamia nuts,
   toasted

Preparation of the Pasta
■ Cook the pasta according to instructions on the package.

Preparation of the Macadamia Paste
■ Blend the macadamia nuts in a food processor. Slowly add the olive oil, and blend the ingredients until they turn into a creamy paste. Adjust the amount of oil as needed.

Preparation of the Chicken and Sauce
■ In a non-stick pan, sauté the chicken in the olive oil over medium-high heat for 5 minutes, until it turns golden brown.
■ Add the salt and pepper to taste. Add the garlic, mushrooms, sun-dried tomatoes and basil, and sauté the mixture for 5 minutes.
■ Flame the pan with brandy. Add ¼ cup of the macadamia paste, then add the half-and-half. Cook the mixture for 5 minutes, and remove the pan from the heat.
■ Toss the mixture with the parmesan.

Assembly
■ Toss the pasta with the sauce.
■ Garnish the mixture with the macadamia nuts.

Lattaiolo

The Italian chef's answer to crème brûlée. Serves 6.

Ingredients

2 or 3 drops almond oil
4 eggs
⅓ cup granulated sugar
2 or 3 drops vanilla extract
2 cups milk

Assembly

- Preheat the oven to 350 degrees F.
- Brush a 9-inch ring mold with the almond oil.
- Beat the eggs, sugar and vanilla in a medium bowl, until they are well-blended and the mixture thickens. Beat in the milk, and mix gradually.
- Pour the egg mixture into the prepared pan. Place the mold in a baking dish. Pour water into the dish to a depth of 1 inch.
- Bake the custard for 20 minutes. Cover the mold with aluminum foil, and bake for 40 minutes, until the custard has set.
- Remove the custard from the oven, and let it cool slightly.
- Run a knife blade around the edges of the pan to loosen the custard. Invert the custard onto a serving plate, and let it cool completely.
- Serve cold.

Wine Suggestion

Taurino, Salice Salentino Rosato, Apulia, Italy, *or*
Castello di Monte Antico, Tuscany, Italy

Italy Meets Hawaii

Roy Yamaguchi

Roasted Eggplant Soup with Ginger and Basil

Warm Salad of Puna Goat Cheese with Roasted Peppers, Shallots and

 Balsamic Vinaigrette

Roy's Asian Primavera Pasta

Lilikoi (Passion Fruit) Tart

S O U P

Roasted Eggplant Soup with Ginger and Basil

Widely used in the Italian kitchen, eggplant assumes an Asian flair in this recipe through the addition of ginger root and fresh basil leaves. You may serve the soup either hot or cold. Serves 6.

Eggplant
1 pound whole eggplant

Soup
¼ cup olive oil
3 cloves garlic, minced
½ cup chopped onions
½ cup chopped carrots
½ cup chopped celery
1 tablespoon minced ginger
2 tomatoes, chopped
1 red bell pepper, chopped
1 quart water
2 tablespoons julienned basil
Salt and pepper to taste

Preparation of the Eggplant
■ Heat the oven to 350 degrees F.
■ Place the whole eggplant in the oven and roast it for 25 to 30 minutes, until it is soft.
■ Remove the eggplant from the oven. Let it cool, then chop it into bite-size pieces.

Preparation of the Soup
■ Heat the olive oil in a large soup pot over medium heat. Sauté the garlic, onions, carrots, celery, ginger, tomatoes and bell pepper in the pot for 2 minutes.
■ Add the water, eggplant and basil, and simmer the mixture for 15 minutes.
■ Puree the vegetables and liquid in a food mill or food processor.
■ Adjust the seasoning with salt and pepper.

Roy's Asian Primavera Pasta

Warm Salad of Puna Goat Cheese with Roasted Peppers, Shallots and Balsamic Vinaigrette

Roy Yamaguchi turns to a family-run business in Puna (an eastern district of the Big Island) to buy his goat cheese, which he likes because it is well-textured, creamy and mild. Serves 4.

Bell Peppers
1 whole red bell pepper
1 whole yellow bell pepper

Eggplant and Shallots
4 shallots, quartered
¼ cup olive oil
1 teaspoon minced garlic
1 cup diced eggplant
Salt and pepper to taste

Preparation of the Bell Peppers
- Place the red and yellow peppers over an open flame for 5 minutes, turning frequently, until they are charred.
- Cover the peppers with plastic wrap, and steam them for 1 hour.
- Using your fingers, peel the skin off the peppers. Wash them briefly under running water, and remove the seeds.
- Julienne the peppers, and set aside.

Preparation of the Eggplant and Shallots
- Sauté the shallots in the oil over medium-high heat for 1 minute.
- Add the garlic, and cook the mixture for 15 seconds.
- Add the eggplant, and brown the mixture thoroughly for 2 minutes. Season with the salt and pepper.
- Remove the mixture from the pan, and set aside.

Vinaigrette

6 tablespoons olive oil
½ teaspoon minced garlic
½ teaspoon minced shallots
¼ cup balsamic vinegar
1 cup basil, julienned

Salad

7½ cups salad mix
6 ounces goat cheese, cut into 4 portions

Preparation of the Vinaigrette

■ Heat the olive oil in a sauté pan. Add the garlic and shallots, and brown them over moderate heat for 15 seconds.
■ Add the balsamic vinegar and basil. Cook the mixture for 30 seconds.
■ Remove the vinaigrette from the heat, and set aside.

Assembly of the Salad

■ In a salad bowl, combine the salad mix with the sautéed eggplant and roasted bell peppers.
■ Add the vinaigrette, and mix the ingredients thoroughly.
■ Divide the salad evenly among 4 plates. Place the goat cheese around or on top of the salad.

Roy's Asian Primavera Pasta

This healthy, well-balanced primavera—the Italian word for spring—combines fresh Hawaii-grown vegetables with Asian seasonings such as ginger and lemongrass. Serves 4.

Ingredients

½ pound uncooked linguine, or ramen noodles
3 tablespoons olive oil
1 tablespoon sesame oil
1 cup cubed fresh shiitake mushrooms
¼ cup rehydrated sun-dried tomatoes
½ cup chopped scallions
24 baby florets of broccoli, lightly blanched
½ red bell pepper, diced
½ cup whole snow peas
½ cup bean sprouts
½ cup julienned carrots
1 tablespoon minced ginger
1 tablespoon chopped garlic
1 tablespoon minced lemongrass stalk
1 cup chopped spinach leaves
Soy sauce to taste

Garnish

¼ cup kaiware sprouts
4 teaspoons Japanese plum sauce
1 teaspoon sesame seeds or
¼ cup goat cheese

Preparation

■ Prepare the noodles according to the directions on the package. Cook the noodles until they are al dente, and drain them.

Assembly

■ Heat 1 tablespoon of the olive oil and all of the sesame oil in a sauté pan. Add the mushrooms, sun-dried tomatoes, scallions, broccoli, peppers, peas, bean sprouts and carrots. Toss well while sautéeing for 45 seconds to 1 minute.

■ Create an opening in the middle of the sauté pan, and place the ginger, garlic, lemongrass and 1 tablespoon of the olive oil in the opening. Sauté the ginger, garlic and lemongrass mixture for 30 seconds, then toss it with the rest of the vegetables.

■ Add the noodles to the vegetables in the sauté pan. Add the spinach and sauté it for 30 seconds. Add the remaining 1 tablespoon of olive oil and the soy sauce.

■ Place the pasta-vegetable mixture into 4 soup bowls.

■ Garnish with kaiware sprouts, Japanese plums, sesame seeds or goat cheese.

Lilikoi (Passion Fruit) Tart

While he prefers the tangy pulp of the lilikoi (passion fruit) for this tart, Chef Yamaguchi says that orange or lemon juice are appropriate substitutes. Serves 6 to 8.

Dough
2 cups pastry flour
1 stick plus 3 tablespoons butter
$\frac{1}{3}$ cup granulated sugar
1 egg yolk

Filling
2 large whole eggs
3 medium-size egg yolks
$\frac{3}{4}$ cup plus 2 tablespoons sugar
Grated rind of 1 orange
$\frac{1}{2}$ cup plus 3 tablespoons fresh lilikoi (passion fruit) pulp, or orange or lemon juice
1 stick unsalted butter, softened

Preparation of the Dough
- Preheat the oven to 350 degrees F.
- Place all the ingredients in a food processor, and blend them for 1 minute, until they form a ball.
- Remove the dough, and refrigerate it for 30 minutes.
- Roll the dough to $\frac{1}{8}$-inch thickness. Place it in a 9-inch tart shell, and bake for 10 to 15 minutes. Remove the shell from the oven, and let it cool.

Preparation of the Filling
- Combine the eggs, egg yolks, sugar, orange rind and passion fruit pulp in a medium stainless-steel bowl. Whisk the mixture to break it down and smooth the egg yolks.
- Place the bowl over a double boiler, and whisk the mixture for 3 to 5 minutes, until it becomes very thick.
- Add the butter, and whisk the mixture until the butter is fully incorporated.

Assembly
- Pour the filling evenly into the shell as quickly as possible.
- Refrigerate the dessert for 1 hour before serving.

Wine Suggestion
Schloss Saarstein, Riesling Kabinett, Saar, Germany

Hawaii Seafood

Time was when the ubiquitous mahimahi (dolphinfish—not related to dolphins) and opakapaka (pink snapper) defined Hawaii seafood. Now, while still highly prized, they share the spotlight with dozens of other fish varieties that are fast gaining acceptance on island menus.

Hawaii chefs have learned the subtle distinctions between the flavors and textures of today's catch. They buy ahi (yellowfin or bigeye tuna), slice it thin and serve it raw as sashimi dipped in wasabi (horse-radish) and soy sauce. They grill aku (skipjack tuna) and serve it with sesame-ginger sauce. They stir-fry kajiki (blue marlin) and present it with macadamia nuts and taro chips. They incorporate the lean, white, medium-dense flesh of the hapuupuu (Hawaiian sea bass or grouper) into a fish stew. They concoct a Thai lobster curry sauce for seared shutome (swordfish) and a papaya basil sauce for steamed opah (moonfish).

At the same time, farmed seafood has become a common ingredient in Hawaii recipes. Aquacultural ponds in North Shore Oahu turn out fresh, plump shrimp for a salad with mango, grapes and a sweet-sour coconut vinaigrette. And at Keahole, on the Big Island, giant tanks of cold, deep-sea water cultivate abalone, lobsters, oysters, salmon and the main ingredient of an ogo (seaweed)-tomato relish.

Smoked Marlin Potato Skins with Sour Cream and Tobiko (Flying Fish Roe), accompanied by Green Papaya Salad

Roasted Swordfish

Jean-Marie Josselin

Smoked Marlin Potato Skins with Sour Cream and Tobiko (Flying Fish Roe)

Green Papaya Salad

Roasted Shutome (Swordfish) with Coriander Scallion Pesto Served with

　　Galangha (Thai Ginger) Lemongrass Broth and Glassy Noodles

Macadamia Nut Tarts with Coconut Cream

APPETIZER
Smoked Marlin Potato Skins with Sour Cream and Tobiko

Jean-Marie Josselin accentuates the flavors of smoky marlin and mild potato with a garnish of crunchy tobiko (flying fish roe). Smoked tuna or salmon may be substituted for the marlin. Makes 1 serving of 4 skins.

Filling
3 tablespoons chopped ginger
1 tablespoon minced garlic
1 teaspoon olive oil
1 carrot, cut in small julienne
1 zucchini, cut in small julienne
3 ounces smoked marlin, julienned
3 tablespoons oyster sauce

Potato Skins
2 whole new red potatoes
1 quart oil for deep-frying

Garnish
$1/2$ cup sour cream
3 tablespoons tobiko (flying fish roe)
1 scallion, cut in small julienne

Preparation of the Filling
■ In a skillet, sauté the ginger and garlic in the olive oil for 30 seconds.
■ Add the carrot and zucchini and sauté them for 20 seconds, until they are soft.
■ Add the marlin and cook for 1 minute more.
■ Mix in the oyster sauce and set aside.

Preparation of the Potato Skins
■ Cut the potatoes in half, lengthwise and empty the centers with a spoon. Deep-fry the skins in the oil for about 5 minutes or until they are cooked.

Assembly
■ Place some of the filling in the center of each potato. Top with the sour cream, tobiko and scallions.

54

Green Papaya Salad

Derived from Thailand, green papaya salad is made out of a fruit with a starchy consistency and a refreshing crunch. Serves 4.

Ingredients

1 medium green papaya
1 large cucumber
2 medium carrots
1 teaspoon minced garlic
2 teaspoons chopped fresh cilantro
1 teaspoon sugar
Juice of 2 limes
Salt and pepper

Preparation

- Peel the papaya and, using a grater, shred the pulp finely. Discard the seeds.
- Peel the cucumber and carrots, then grate them.

Assembly

- In a medium bowl, combine the papaya, cucumber and carrots. Add the garlic, cilantro, sugar and lime juice.
- Season to taste with the salt and pepper. Chill before serving.

Roasted Shutome with Coriander Scallion Pesto Served with Galangha Lemongrass Broth and Glassy Noodles

Shutome, the swordfish caught off Hawaii's shores, is also called by its Hawaiian name, a'u. Serves 2.

Shutome

12 ounces shutome (swordfish), or marlin,
   cut into 4 (3-ounce) medallions
Salt and pepper to taste

Pesto

1/4 cup coriander seeds
1/4 cup fresh ground ginger
1 cup chopped scallions
1 cup basil, stems removed
1/4 cup roasted Hawaiian macadamia nuts
1 cup extra-virgin olive oil

Preparation of the Shutome

- Season the shutome with salt and pepper. Refrigerate it until it is time to assemble the dish.

Preparation of the Pesto

- Combine all the ingredients, except the olive oil. Process the mixture in the blender for a few seconds.
- Slowly add the olive oil, until the mixture looks like a chunky paste.

Broth

1½ cups fish stock
4 pieces galangha (Thai ginger), or regular ginger
4 stalks lemongrass

Mushrooms

2 cups medium-sliced chanterelle or shiitake
   mushrooms
2 teaspoons olive oil
Salt and pepper to taste

Noodles

1 (8-ounce) package bean thread noodles

Assembly

¼ cup oil

Preparation of the Broth
- Place the fish stock in a saucepan. Add the galangha and lemongrass and cook them slowly for 20 minutes, until the stock is strong in flavor.
- Stir in the salt and pepper, and remove from the heat.

Preparation of the Mushrooms
- Sauté the mushrooms in the oil for 30 seconds. Add the salt and pepper, and set aside until ready to use.

Preparation of the Noodles
- In a bowl, cover the noodles in water and soak them for 1 hour. Drain noodles before serving.

Assembly
- Spoon 1 tablespoon of pesto on each piece of fish.
- Heat the oil in a non-stick skillet over medium heat. Sauté the fish in the skillet, pesto-side down first. Cook the fish for about 3 minutes on each side or until it is medium-rare.
- Place the noodles on the center of a plate. Add the mushrooms artfully around the noodles. Place the medallions of fish on the noodles and finish with the broth.

DESSERT

Macadamia Nut Tarts with Coconut Cream

Josselin admits that in creating this dessert he was looking for something that tastes like a Milky Way candy bar. Makes 8 tarts.

Pastry

1⅓ cups flour
¼ cup super-fine sugar
Pinch of salt
1 stick unsalted butter, chilled
½ beaten egg
¼ cup grated fresh coconut

Preparation of the Pastry
- Preheat the oven to 350 degrees F.
- Mix the flour, sugar and salt in a medium bowl. Grate the butter into the bowl. Blend the ingredients with your fingers or process them until you have a mealy crumb mixture.
- Mix in the egg and coconut to cohere the dough. You may need to add a bit more flour.

Filling
1 cup super-fine sugar
½ cup heavy cream
8 ounces Hawaiian macadamia nut pieces,
   lightly toasted

Topping
2 cups heavy cream
½ cup grated toasted coconut

- Cover and chill the dough for at least 1 hour.
- Roll out the dough and line 8 (4-inch) tins with it. Bake the tart shells for 5 minutes. Prick the bases with a fork and bake another 5 minutes.

Preparation of the Filling
- Put ¼ cup of the sugar into a heavy pan and melt it over low heat, stirring. Add the rest of the sugar, tablespoon by tablespoon, and stir it over the heat for 10 to 15 minutes, until it caramelizes to a golden brown.
- Gradually pour in the cream. The mixture may turn lumpy; keep stirring until it is smooth.
- Mix in the nuts, cooking gently for 2 minutes. They should be thoroughly coated.

Assembly
- Fill the tart shells with the nut mixture and return them to the oven until the pastry is nicely browned, about 5 minutes more.
- The tarts may be served warm or cold. When ready to serve, whip the cream until stiff, fold in the toasted coconut, and put a dollop on each tart.

Wine Suggestion
Kermit Lynch (Importer), Vouvray, Loire Valley, France

Distinctive Mahimahi

Roy Yamaguchi

Carpaccio of Beef with Arugula and Sesame Soy Vinaigrette

Salad of Seafood Tortellini with Pine Nuts and Pan-Roasted Tomatoes

Mahimahi (Dolphinfish) with Goat Cheese Hash

Tropical Fruit Crème Brûlée with Candied Ginger

APPETIZER

Carpaccio of Beef with Arugula and Sesame Soy Vinaigrette

Carpaccio, very thin slices of raw beef, is an Italian specialty; Yamaguchi gives it a Hawaii twist by drizzling it with an Asian-style sauce. Serves 4.

Ingredients

¼ pound beef tenderloin
8 baby artichokes, sliced
½ tablespoon olive oil
½ tablespoon sesame oil
¼ teaspoon minced garlic
¼ teaspoon minced ginger
3¾ cups baby arugula, or other baby lettuce
1¼ cups radicchio, or red cabbage, chopped in bite-size pieces
1 tablespoon soy sauce
1 tablespoon olive oil
⅛ cup parmesan cheese, thinly sliced

Preparation of the Beef

■ Cut the beef into 2-ounce portions. Flatten them until they are very thin and place them around the plate.

Assembly

■ Over medium heat, sauté the artichokes in the olive oil and sesame oil for about 1 minute.
■ When the artichokes become a little crispy, add the garlic and ginger and sauté for about 10 seconds.
■ Add the arugula and radicchio and toss them in the skillet for about 10 seconds to fully coat them with the oil mixture.
■ Immediately place the mixture over the beef. Drizzle the soy sauce and olive oil over the beef and garnish it with the cheese.

Mahimahi (Dolphinfish) with Goat Cheese Hash

Salad of Seafood Tortellini with Pine Nuts and Pan-Roasted Tomatoes

In this recipe, Yamaguchi calls for the Roma tomato, an Italian variety which is very good when cooked. If Roma isn't available, he suggests substituting any type of plump, ripe tomato. Serves 4.

Tortellini Filling
1½ ounces prosciutto, minced
6 ounces shrimp, coarsely chopped
6 ounces scallops, coarsely chopped
⅛ teaspoon minced garlic
¼ teaspoon minced basil

Spinach Mixture
1¾ cups spinach leaf
¼ cup diced fresh shiitake mushrooms
⅛ teaspoon minced garlic
2 tablespoons olive oil
¼ cup ricotta cheese

Salad
6 cups baby salad mix
1 teaspoon olive oil
Salt to taste

Pan-Roasted Tomatoes
2 tablespoons olive oil
2½ Roma tomatoes, sliced lengthwise
   into 8 (½-inch thick) slices

Cabernet Sauce
1 medium onion, chopped
1 carrot, chopped
1 celery, chopped
4 bay leaves
5 black peppercorns
8 whole garlic cloves
¼ cup cooking oil
⅛ ounce sugar
4 cups cabernet
4 cups veal stock

Preparation of the Tortellini Filling
■ Combine all the ingredients in a medium bowl and set aside.

Preparation of the Spinach Mixture
■ In a very hot skillet, sauté the spinach, mushrooms and garlic in the oil for about 30 seconds or until the spinach is fully cooked.
■ Remove the mixture from the pan. Squeeze out any excess liquid and chop the spinach. Place the spinach in a medium bowl and stir in the ricotta until it is mixed. Add this mixture to the tortellini filling.

Preparation of the Salad
■ Coat the salad mix with the olive oil and season it with salt.

Preparation of the Pan-Roasted Tomatoes
■ In a very hot skillet in olive oil, sauté the tomatoes 45 seconds per side, until they are nicely browned or even close to being charred.

Preparation of the Cabernet Sauce
■ In a saucepan, slowly sauté the onions, carrots, celery, bay leaves, peppercorns and garlic in cooking oil for about 5 minutes over medium heat or until the vegetables are golden brown.
■ Add the sugar and caramelize the mixture for about 2 minutes while stirring.
■ Deglaze with the red wine and reduce the mixture by ⅔, to 2 cups, approximately 15 to 20 minutes.
■ Add the veal stock and reduce the mixture by ⅔, approximately 15 to 20 minutes, then strain.
■ Reduce the mixture 2 to 5 minutes more, until it coats the back of a spoon.

Tortellini

2 tablespoons cornstarch

2 tablespoons water

20 pot sticker wrappers

Garnish

1 tablespoon roasted pine nuts

Preparation of the Tortellini

■ Dissolve the cornstarch in the water.

■ Place a pot sticker wrapper on a flat surface. Place ½ teaspoon of the tortellini/spinach filling in the middle of the wrapper. Brush the cornstarch water around the edges of the wrapper.

■ Fold over the wrapper to form a half-moon and seal the edges tight. Wrap the half-moon around your index finger like a ring (the straight edge side away from you). Cement the two edges with your thumb.

■ Place the tortellini in a pot of boiling water and cook for 2 minutes, or until they float up to the surface.

Assembly

■ Place 5 tortellini in a soup bowl and place 2 tomatoes on top of the tortellini. Pour about ¼ cup of sauce over the tomatoes and place the salad mixture over the tomatoes. Sprinkle with the nuts.

ENTREE

Mahimahi with Goat Cheese Hash

Best-known of the Hawaiian fishes, mahimahi (dolphinfish) is in no way related to the marine mammal. It has a moist, sweet, light pink flesh that cooks to white. Serves 4.

Red Wine Sauce

1 onion, chopped

1 large carrot, chopped

1 cup chopped celery

1 tablespoon peppercorns

1 bay leaf

2 tablespoons sugar

2 cups red wine

2 cups veal stock

Preparation of Red Wine Sauce

■ Place the onions, carrots, celery, peppercorns, bay leaf and sugar in a saucepan over medium heat. Caramelize the mixture for 3 to 5 minutes, until it turns deep brown.

■ Add the red wine and reduce by ⅔, for 15 to 20 minutes.

■ Add the veal stock and reduce by ⅔, to 2½ cups, for 15 to 20 minutes.

■ Strain the mixture and set aside warm.

Preparation of the Goat Cheese Hash

■ Sauté the mushrooms in 1 tablespoon of the oil over high heat for 45 seconds. Reduce the heat to medium, add the garlic and sauté the mixture for 15 seconds.

Goat Cheese Hash

1 cup julienned fresh shiitake mushrooms
2 tablespoons olive oil
½ teaspoon minced garlic
1 cup fresh spinach leaves
3 cups mashed potatoes
¼ cup julienned basil leaves
¼ cup sun-dried tomatoes
½ cup broccoli florets, cooked al dente
½ cup goat cheese
Salt and pepper to taste

Mahimahi

Salt and pepper to taste
2 (8-ounce) mahimahi (dolphinfish) fillets, or
   snapper
2 tablespoons olive oil

Salad Mix

Salt and pepper to taste
1 teaspoon red wine vinegar
2 teaspoons olive oil
1 cup baby salad greens

Shoestring Potatoes

1 large potato, julienned
2 cups oil for frying

■ Add the spinach and toss until the leaves are slightly wilted, 15 to 20 seconds. Remove the mixture from the pan and place the ingredients in a large bowl.

■ Add the mashed potatoes, basil, sun-dried tomatoes, broccoli, goat cheese, salt and pepper. Mix until the ingredients are well incorporated.

■ Form the mixture into 3-inch pancakes and pan-fry them in the remaining oil. Cook the pancakes 1 to 1½ minutes per side, until they are lightly brown.

Preparation of the Mahimahi

■ Lightly salt and pepper each side of the mahimahi and coat it with olive oil.

■ Place the mahimahi into a hot sauté pan and sear it 1 minute per side, until it is medium-rare to medium in doneness.

Preparation of the Salad Mix

■ Add the salt, pepper, vinegar and olive oil to the greens and toss them until they are well mixed.

Preparation of the Shoestring Potatoes

■ Fry the potatoes in oil for 5 minutes until they are crispy brown. Drain and dry them on a paper towel.

Assembly

■ Place the goat cheese hash on the center of a plate and lay the mahimahi over the hash.

■ Add ½ cup of salad greens over each fillet and top them with a garnish of shoestring potatoes.

■ Surround the assembled ingredients with the red wine sauce.

Tropical Fruit Crème Brûlée with Candied Ginger

For this dish, which can be served warm (not hot) or cold, always work with the freshest fruit of the season. Yamaguchi recommends using raspberries, pineapples, mangoes or papayas. Serves 6.

Candied Ginger
1/4 cup finely diced fresh ginger
2 cups water
1/4 cup sugar

Crème Brûlée
1 quart milk
1 cup sugar
I vanilla bean, split lengthwise
9 eggs
2 yolks
1/4 cup lilikoi (passion fruit) syrup, or orange juice concentrate

Tropical Fruit
3 cups fresh fruit, chopped in bite-sized pieces

Preparation of the Candied Ginger
- Place the ginger in a sauté pan and fill it with 1 cup of water.
- Bring it to a boil and discard the water.
- Fill the pan again with 1 cup of water and add the sugar. Reduce the mixture slowly for 5 minutes, until it reaches a syrup consistency.

Preparation of the Crème Brûlée
- Warm the milk, sugar and vanilla in a medium pot for 5 minutes. Remove the pot from heat.
- Whip the eggs and yolks by hand in a small bowl for 2 minutes, just until thoroughly mixed.
- Add ½ cup of the warm milk to the eggs. Mix, then strain back into the pot.
- Add the passion fruit syrup and stir slowly. Remove the pot from the heat.
- Let the mixture set for 10 minutes, then skim off the foam on top.

Assembly
- Preheat the oven to 350 degrees F.
- Place a tablespoon each of the candied ginger and fruit mixture on the bottom of a 5- to 6-ounce bowl that can bake in the oven.
- Fill the bowl to the top and repeat the process with the other bowls.
- Set the bowls in a pan that can be filled with water at least ⅓ up the sides of the bowls.
- Bake on the middle rack 35 to 40 minutes until the filling has set.
- Sprinkle a liberal amount of sugar on top of the crème brûlée and burn it with a household propane torch.

Wine Suggestion
Domaine Tempier, Rosé, Bandol, France, *or*
Charles Joquet, Chinon, Loire, France

Chinatown

At a Hong Kong-style herbalist shop in downtown Honolulu, hundreds of tiny bottles and drawers are filled with restorative potions—anise, snake oil and dried sea horse. Next door, an acupuncturist practices therapeutic centuries-old traditions believed to cure everything from allergies to whiplash. Nearby, a 19th-century temple provides a peaceful retreat for families who pray over lighted candles.

Welcome to Honolulu's Chinatown, where every morning the streets come alive with shoppers haggling over groceries and imported goods in the chatter of foreign languages, and every evening the neon signs flash over funky nightclubs dating back to World War II.

Within its 15 square blocks, Oahu's Chinatown possesses treasures both cultural and culinary. Its centerpiece is Oahu Market, in operation since 1904. In this open-air food emporium with a tin roof, pig heads vie for attention with roast ducks. Butchers stand behind displays of fresh beef and raw fish with their knives poised, while mango, lychee and cherimoya (pinecone-shaped fruits with tart white meat) brighten up the fruit stands. And, due to the more recent influx of Thai, Vietnamese, Cambodian and Laotian immigrants to this area, you're as apt to encounter a bowl of pho (Vietnamese soup) and a plate of mee krob (Thai noodle salad) as you are a heaping order of Chinese chop suey.

Crispy Asian Spring Rolls with Chili Plum Sauce, accompanied by Spicy Grilled Shrimp Salad with Fresh Tropical Fruits

Flavor of Chinatown

Roy Yamaguchi

Crispy Asian Spring Rolls with Chili Plum Sauce

Spicy Grilled Shrimp Salad with Fresh Tropical Fruits

New Chinatown Duck

White Chocolate Candied Ginger Ice Cream

APPETIZER

Crispy Asian Spring Rolls with Chili Plum Sauce

Bean thread noodles are made from mung beans; they become transparent when rehydrated, which explains their nickname, cellophane noodles. Makes 10 spring rolls.

Beef Mixture

2 tablespoons sesame oil
2 tablespoons salad oil
1 pound ground tenderloin
1 tablespoon chopped ginger
1 tablespoon chopped garlic
1 tablespoon chopped lemongrass
5 kaffir lime leaves (Asian lime leaf), minced
1 tablespoon freshly ground black pepper
½ tablespoon fish sauce

Shrimp Mixture

1 tablespoon salad oil
1 tablespoon sesame oil
1½ pounds large shrimp, diced
Black pepper to taste
¼ cup sliced lemongrass stalks

Preparation of the Beef Mixture

■ Heat the sesame and salad oil in a large pan. Sauté the beef for 2 minutes.
■ Add the ginger, garlic, lemongrass and lime leaves. Season with the pepper. Add the fish sauce.
■ Place the mixture on a plate and tilt plate to drain the oil. Set aside.

Preparation of the Shrimp Mixture

■ Heat the salad oil and sesame oil and sauté the shrimp for about 30 seconds.
■ Add the pepper and lemongrass stalks.
■ Toss the mixture for 30 seconds.
■ Remove the lemongrass stalks and set the mixture aside.

Vegetable Mixture

1/4 cup black fungus mushrooms, soaked
    overnight and julienned
1 tablespoon sesame oil
1 tablespoon salad oil
1 cup grated carrot
1 cup fresh bean sprouts
3 kaffir lime leaves, thinly sliced
1/2 tablespoon fresh ground black pepper

Chili Plum Sauce

3 very ripe plums, seeded and chopped
1/2 orange
1/2 cup sake
1/2 cup plum wine
1/2 cup Lingham chili sauce or any syrupy,
    spicy/sweet sauce
1/2 cup chopped cilantro

Spring Rolls

1 (4-ounce) bag bean thread noodles, or rice
    noodles
1 cup chopped basil
1 tablespoon chopped lemongrass
1 whole egg
1 package 8-inch Bang Thrang rice paper
1 beaten egg for egg wash
Cornstarch for dusting
2 cups oil for frying

Garnish

Italian parsley
Sesame seeds

Preparation of the Vegetable Mixture

■ Heat the sesame and salad oil in a medium sauté pan.
■ Add the carrots, bean sprouts and black fungus mushrooms. Add the lime leaves and season with the pepper.
■ Cook the mixture for about 1 minute. Place it on a plate to cool.

Preparation of the Chili Plum Sauce

■ Place the plums in a saucepan. Add the orange, sake, plum wine and chili sauce. Add the cilantro and cook for 30 minutes at low heat.
■ Strain the sauce and serve at room temperature.

Assembly

■ Cook the noodles in a saucepan of boiling water for 5 to 10 minutes, until they are soft. Drain them extremely well.
■ Chop the noodles coarsely and place them into a large bowl. Add the basil, lemongrass, meat mixture, shrimp mixture, vegetable mixture and 1 egg, and combine the ingredients well.
■ Dip the rice paper in warm water, drain any excess water, and lay the paper out flat.
■ Fill the paper with 2 tablespoons of the spring roll mixture. Brush the edges of the paper with the egg wash. Roll the filled paper into the shape of a burrito. Seal the ends and dust with cornstarch.
■ Fry each spring roll in hot oil for about 45 seconds on each side or until it turns golden brown. Cut each spring roll in half.
■ Place about 1/4 cup of the chili plum sauce on each plate, and place the spring rolls, cut side up, on the plate.
■ Garnish with the parsley and sesame seeds.

Spicy Grilled Shrimp Salad with Fresh Tropical Fruits

Roy Yamaguchi prefers the spicy flavors of watercress and mizuna in this salad. If those greens are not available, however, he recommends substituting a baby lettuce mix. Serves 4.

Salad Mix
2½ ounces watercress leaves
2½ ounces mizuna

Shrimp
16 (16-20 size) shrimp
¼ cup Lingham chili sauce, or any Asian chili sauce
½ tablespoon minced lemongrass
1 teaspoon minced garlic
1 teaspoon minced shallots
1 teaspoon minced ginger
2 teaspoons roasted white sesame seeds

Fruit
½ green papaya, julienned
½ mango, julienned
½ cup cucumbers, skin on, no seeds, julienned

Dressing
½ cup sour cream
½ cup heavy cream, whipped
1 tablespoon orange juice concentrate
Juice of ½ lemon
1 teaspoon minced chives
1 tablespoon lilikoi (passion fruit) syrup

Preparation of the Salad Mix
■ Toss watercress and mizuna in a medium bowl and set aside.

Preparation of the Shrimp
■ Combine all the ingredients in a large bowl and marinate the shrimp for 10 minutes.
■ Grill the shrimp about 1 minute on each side until they are done.

Preparation of the Fruit
■ Combine all the ingredients in a medium bowl. Set aside.

Preparation of the Dressing
■ Combine all the ingredients in a medium bowl and mix well. Set aside.

Assembly
■ Spread ¼ cup of the dressing on each plate.
■ Place 1 cup of the salad mix on each plate.
■ Add the mixed fruits on top of the watercress and mizuna.
■ Arrange 4 shrimps on top of the fruit on each plate.

New Chinatown Duck

Yamaguchi calls for dried shiitake mushrooms because their earthy, pungent flavor provides an ideal counterpart to the strong, spicy marinade. Serves 4.

Ducks and Marinade

1 tablespoon minced garlic
1 tablespoon minced ginger
1 cup soy sauce
2 cups hoisin sauce
1 tablespoon Lanchi chili sauce, or any garlic chili paste
2 cups sherry
1 cup honey
1 green onion, chopped fine
2 whole, uncooked ducks

Vegetable Garnish

2 tablespoons olive oil
1/2 pound dried shiitake mushrooms, soaked overnight and julienned
2 baby bok choy leaves, or Napa cabbage leaves
16 fresh water chestnuts, sliced
1/2 cup dried black fungus mushrooms, soaked overnight and julienned
1/2 cup (1-inch strips) green onion
Minced ginger to taste
Lanchi chili sauce to taste

Preparation of the Ducks and Marinade

■ Mix the garlic, ginger, soy sauce, hoisin sauce, chili sauce, sherry, honey and green onion in a large bowl. Add the ducks and marinate for 1 day.
■ Preheat the oven to 350 degrees F.
■ Roast the duck on a rack for about 1 hour.

Preparation of the Vegetable Garnish

■ Heat the oil and sauté the shiitake mushrooms, bok choy, water chestnuts, black fungus mushrooms, green onions, ginger and chili sauce in a large pan over medium heat.
■ Cook the mixture for 30 seconds, until the bok choy is slightly wilted.

Assembly

■ Remove the leg and breast of the ducks.
■ Slice the breast into three pieces and serve it with the vegetables.

White Chocolate Candied Ginger Ice Cream

While dark chocolate can be used in this recipe, Yamaguchi believes white chocolate provides a better complement to the spicy/sweet candied ginger. Serves 6.

Candied Ginger
¼ cup finely diced ginger
2 cups water
¼ cup sugar

Ice Cream
2 pints milk
2 pints cream
½ cup minced mint leaves
14 ounces white chocolate, cut into 1-inch pieces
8 egg yolks

Preparation of the Candied Ginger
- Place the ginger in a medium sauté pan and fill it with 1 cup of water. Bring it to a boil and discard the water.
- Fill the pan back up with 1 cup of water, add the sugar and reduce it over low heat for 10 minutes or until it reaches a syrup consistency.

Preparation of the Ice Cream
- In a large saucepan, scald the milk and cream together with the mint leaves for 3 minutes. Remove the pot from the heat.
- Let the mixture sit for 30 minutes, then strain it. Reserve the cream for later use.
- In a double boiler, melt the chocolate over extremely low heat and reserve it for later use.
- In a large bowl, whisk the egg yolks for about 1 minute until they are smooth.
- Reheat the cream to scalding. Add ⅓ of the cream to the yolks and whisk them together. Return this mixture to the saucepan with the remaining cream.
- Stir the cream with a wooden spoon over low heat for 10 to 15 minutes, until it thickens and coats the back of the spoon. Strain the cream and pour in the melted chocolate and ¼ cup of the candied ginger. Keep stirring to incorporate the ingredients well.
- Pour the mixture into a bowl and chill it for 1 hour.
- Pour the mixture into an ice cream maker. Follow the instructions on the ice cream maker to finish the dessert.

Wine Suggestion
Pfeffingen Riesling Spatlese, Ungsteiner Herrenberg, Rheinpfalz, Germany

Peking Duck Plus
Roy Yamaguchi

Lemongrass Chicken (or Beef) with Linguine

Roasted Peking-Style Duck with Candied Pecans in a Lilikoi (Passion Fruit) Sauce

Chocolate Coconut Macadamia Nut Tart

SIDE DISH

Lemongrass Chicken (or Beef) with Linguine

Available in Asian markets, lemongrass is a fragrant herb that grows in abundance in the tropics. Work with the white part of the stalk. Serves 4.

Marinade
1 teaspoon minced shallots
2 tablespoons minced lemongrass
2 teaspoons olive oil
1 teaspoon sesame oil
1/2 teaspoon minced ginger
1/4 teaspoon minced garlic
1 tablespoon soy sauce

Meat
1 pound boneless chicken breast or
   New York steak

Pasta
6 ounces linguine, uncooked

Preparation of the Marinade
■ In a large bowl, mix all of the ingredients together thoroughly. Set aside.

Preparation of the Meat
■ Marinate the beef or chicken for 1 hour. Grill the meat to your preferred doneness. Remove it from the pan and set aside.

Preparation of the Pasta
■ Cook the linguine in boiling water for 5 minutes, until al dente. Drain it and set aside to cool.

Preparation of the Vegetables
■ Heat the sesame oil and olive oil in a sauté pan. Sauté the bell peppers, peas, cabbage and mushrooms.
■ After about 1 minute, add the ginger and garlic to the pan and cook for 1 minute.

Vegetables

1/2 teaspoon sesame oil
2 1/2 tablespoons olive oil
1/2 cup red bell pepper, julienned
1/2 cup yellow bell pepper, julienned
1 cup Chinese peas, julienned
4 ounces Napa (Chinese) cabbage, julienned
2 1/2 cups fresh shiitake mushrooms
1/4 teaspoon minced ginger
1/4 teaspoon minced garlic
2 teaspoons soy sauce

Garnish

1/4 cup red pickled ginger
1 small container (1/2 cup) Japanese spice
   sprouts (spicy radish sprouts)

■ Add the pasta to the sauté pan and moisten the mixture with the soy sauce.

Assembly

■ Divide the linguine among 4 bowls. Arrange the meat on top of the pasta and garnish it with the ginger and sprouts.

Roasted Peking-Style Duck with Candied Pecans in a Lilikoi Sauce

Roy Yamaguchi skins a duck by inserting an air compressor hose into the cavity and squeezing both ends of the body; chefs at home can accomplish the same task by using their fingers to pull the skin away from the meat. Serves 2.

Marinade

2 cups soy sauce
1 cup hoisin sauce
1 cup honey
1/2 cup chopped ginger
1/4 cup chopped garlic
1/2 cup sugar
6 cups water

Duck

1 (5-pound) duck, whole

Preparation of the Marinade

■ Mix all the ingredients in a large bowl.

Preparation of the Duck

■ Skin the duck by pulling the skin away from the meat with your fingers.
■ Discard the skin and marinate the duck overnight.
■ Preheat the oven to 350 degrees F.
■ Roast the duck in the oven for 1 hour.
■ Cut the duck into pieces, so that there is one leg, thigh and breast per person, and remove the bones.

Lemongrass Chicken with Linguine

Lilikoi Ginger Sauce

2 cups chopped onions
1 cup chopped celery
1 cup chopped carrots
2 whole bay leaves
¼ cup sugar
½ gallon veal stock
5 button mushrooms, julienned
1 medium tomato, chopped
1 quart cabernet sauvignon
1 cup lilikoi (passion fruit) syrup
Pulp of 3 lilikoi, or 2 ounces orange juice
    concentrate
⅛ cup fresh ginger juice
½ teaspoon whole peppercorns

Candied Pecans

¼ cup pecan halves
1 tablespoon butter
1 tablespoon honey

Preparation of the Lilikoi Ginger Sauce

■ In a large saucepan, mix the onions, celery, carrots, bay leaves and sugar and stir constantly over medium heat for 3 to 5 minutes, to caramelize the sauce.

■ Add the veal stock, mushrooms, tomato, cabernet, lilikoi syrup, lilikoi pulp, ginger juice and peppercorns. Continue to reduce the sauce for 30 to 45 minutes to 2 cups, until it starts to coat a spoon.

■ Strain out the vegetables and continue to reduce the stock for 5 to 10 minutes or until it coats the back of a spoon. Yields about 2 cups.

Preparation of the Candied Pecans

■ Sauté the pecans in the butter for 1½ to 2 minutes. When the butter starts to brown, stir in the honey.

■ Remove the mixture from the heat and set aside.

Assembly

■ Slice the duck into thin slices and arrange them on a plate. Spoon ¼ cup of the sauce over the duck and garnish with the candied pecans.

Chocolate Coconut Macadamia Nut Tart

This classic tart, with its tropical flavors of coconut and Hawaiian macadamia nuts, suits Hawaii. Serves 8.

Dough
½ pound pastry flour
½ cup plus 2½ tablespoons butter
¼ cup plus 1½ tablespoons granulated sugar
1 egg yolk

Nut Mixture
¼ cup butter
½ cup brown sugar
¼ cup granulated sugar
1½ tablespoons milk
1 pinch salt
1 ounce semisweet chocolate, finely chopped
1 teaspoon flour
1 egg
1 tablespoon coffee liqueur
1 tablespoon coconut liqueur
1 cup Hawaiian macadamia nuts
½ cup chopped coconut

Garnish
Sweetened whipped cream

Preparation of the Dough
■ Place all the ingredients in a food processor and blend them for 1 minute, until they form a ball.
■ Remove the dough and refrigerate it for 30 minutes.
■ Roll the dough to ⅛-inch thickness. Place it in a 9-inch tart shell and chill it until it is time for assembly.

Preparation of the Nut Mixture
■ Melt the butter in a medium saucepan. Add the sugars, milk and salt, then stir the mixture over low heat for 1 minute until all the ingredients are incorporated.
■ Add the chocolate and stir with a wire whisk until the mixture is very smooth. Remove the pan from the heat and set aside.
■ In a small bowl, mix the flour with the egg and liqueurs.
■ Stir the flour mixture into the chocolate mixture. Stir in the macadamia nuts and coconut, and mix well until all the ingredients are incorporated.

Assembly
■ Preheat the oven to 325 degrees F.
■ Place the nut mixture in the tart shell and bake it for 1 hour. Remove the tart from the oven and cool.
■ Cut the tart into 8 pieces and garnish it with the whipped cream.

Wine Suggestion
Franz Kuenstler Hochheimer Kirchenstuck Spatlese, Rheingau, Germany, *or*
Whitecraft "Olivet Lane" Pinot Noir, Santa Barbara, California

The Big Island of Hawaii

The diverse landscapes of the Big Island charge the imagination. Misty steam vents and canopied rainforests of Hawaii Volcanoes National Park inspire legends about Pele, the volcano goddess. Windswept South Point shorelines conjure up images of 8th-century Polynesians—the island's earliest inhabitants—as they landed their giant voyaging canoes in the crashing surf. Petroglyphs (stone drawings) etched in Puako lava rocks depict early hunting expeditions and battles led by the island's king, Kamehameha the Great. Rolling Waimea ranchlands evoke the longhorns and lariats of 19th-century paniolo (Hawaiian cowboys).

Dominated by 13,679-foot Mauna Loa and 13,796-foot Mauna Kea, the 4,000-square-mile island is a place to think big, and that is precisely what its most successful chefs are doing. They believe in working with ingredients drawn from the fertile land and sea of their vast home. They have developed close associations with local farmers and fishermen, and they brainstorm over fresh-flavored recipes quite unlike any others: Puna goat cheese sushi, Kona seafood chowder, Kahua lamb with mango glaze, Lalamilo strawberry shortcake. Some chefs, like Amy Ferguson-Ota, find their forum for expression in the kitchens of fashionable resorts lining the western Kohala Coast. Other chefs, like Peter Merriman and Sam Choy, have established independent restaurants that help make the Big Island an inventive center of good eating.

Grilled Steak with Roasted Vegetable Sauce accompanied by Green Bean Salad with Maui Onions and Kau Oranges, Orange-Sesame Vinaigrette

A Big Island Picnic

Peter Merriman

Goat Cheese Sushi

Green Bean Salad with Maui Onions and Kau Oranges, Orange-Sesame Vinaigrette

Grilled Steak with Roasted Vegetable Sauce

Macadamia Lace Cookies

APPETIZER
Goat Cheese Sushi

Peter Merriman puts a Hawaii spin on the classic Japanese appetizer. He uses Big Island goat cheese instead of rice, and he wraps the sushi in locally grown arugula instead of nori (dried seaweed). Serves 4.

Goat Cheese Mixture
2 tablespoons virgin olive oil

½ pound Puna goat cheese, or your local goat cheese

¼ cup roasted, crushed Hawaiian macadamia nuts

1 tablespoon cracked black pepper

2 tablespoons chopped pre-soaked sun-dried tomatoes

1 teaspoon salt

1 teaspoon sugar

Preparation of the Goat Cheese Mixture

■ Combine the olive oil, goat cheese, macadamia nuts, pepper, sun-dried tomatoes, salt and sugar in a medium bowl, and mix well.

Assembly

■ Lay a 12-by-16-inch piece of plastic wrap on a work surface. On it, place ¼ of the arugula, top side down, enough to create a 4-by-8-inch rectangle.

■ Place the goat cheese mixture on top of the arugula, enough to spread evenly across the rectangle.

■ Lay ¼ of the bell pepper and eggplant strips down the center of the rectangle.

Assembly

5 cups arugula

1 red bell pepper, roasted, peeled and sliced in thin strips

1 Japanese eggplant, sliced lengthwise in thin strips, dipped in olive oil and grilled

- Roll up the ingredients in the plastic wrap to make a sausage shape, and repeat this process to make 3 more rolls.
- Refrigerate the rolls for 45 minutes to 1 hour.
- Remove the plastic wrap, and slice the sushi 3/4-inch thick.

Green Bean Salad with Maui Onions and Kau Oranges, Orange-Sesame Vinaigrette

A southern district of the Big Island, Kau is well-known for its orange and lime trees, which thrive in the dry, sunny weather of the lava-covered landscape. Serves 4 to 6.

Green Beans

1 pound fresh green beans, stem ends removed

Orange-Sesame Vinaigrette

2 tablespoons honey

1/4 cup soy sauce

1 tablespoon chopped shallots

1 6-ounce can frozen orange juice concentrate

3/4 cup rice wine vinegar, or any delicate vinegar

2 tablespoons grated fresh ginger

1 green onion, thin-sliced

1 tablespoon chopped garlic

2 tablespoons toasted sesame seeds

1/4 cup sesame oil

2 cups vegetable oil

Salt and pepper to taste

Assembly

1 Maui onion, or any sweet onion, cut in half and sliced with the grain

2 large Kau oranges, or Valencia oranges, peeled and divided into wedges

Preparation of the Green Beans

- Place the beans in a small amount of rapidly boiling salted water in a medium saucepan. Return the water to a boil, and cook the beans for 30 seconds.
- Drain the beans, and immediately shock them by submerging them in a large bowl of ice water.

Preparation of the Orange-Sesame Vinaigrette

- Combine the honey, soy sauce, shallots, orange juice, vinegar, ginger, onion, garlic and sesame seeds in a large bowl. Gradually whisk in the oils, and season the vinaigrette with salt and pepper.

Assembly

- Toss the beans, onions and oranges in a large bowl, and dress with the vinaigrette.

Grilled Steak with Roasted Vegetable Sauce

When grilling a steak, make sure the grill is hot enough to sear the outside, keeping the juices inside. The sauce for the following dish can be served either hot or at room temperature. Serves 4.

Roasted Vegetable Sauce
1 red bell pepper
1 carrot, thinly sliced
1 leek, chopped
1 large onion, chopped
2 tomatoes, diced
2 ribs celery, chopped
4 mushrooms, chopped
2 tablespoons olive oil
Salt and pepper
1 shallot, chopped
1 tablespoon olive oil
1$\frac{1}{2}$ cups chicken stock

Garnish
1 Maui onion, or any sweet onion

Steaks
4 (8-ounce) New York steaks

Preparation of the Bell Pepper
- Place the pepper over an open flame (low setting) on a gas burner or, if using an electric stove, as close to the broiling element as possible.
- Cook the pepper 12 to 15 minutes, turning to cook all sides evenly, until it is blackened.
- Remove the pepper from the heat, and place it in a plastic or paper bag to sweat for 20 minutes.
- Remove the pepper from the bag. Use your fingers to peel the skin from the pepper. Remove the stem and seeds and set the pepper aside.

Preparation of the Roasted Vegetable Sauce
- Preheat the oven to 425 degrees F.
- In a medium bowl, toss the carrots, leeks, onions, tomatoes, celery and mushrooms in the oil, and season them with the salt and pepper.
- Spread out the mixture evenly on a roasting pan, and roast for 25 to 30 minutes.
- Sauté the chopped shallots in the oil in a large saucepan for 1 minute. Add the roasted vegetables and chicken stock. Simmer the mixture for 1 to 2 minutes, or until the vegetables are soft.
- Transfer the ingredients to a blender. Add the roasted pepper, and puree the mixture until it reaches your desired consistency.
- Adjust the seasoning to taste, and set aside.

Preparation of the Garnish
- Slice the onion across the grain into 4 thick slices. Grill the slices until your desired doneness, and set aside.

Preparation of the Steaks
- Heavily salt and pepper the steaks, and grill them to your desired doneness.

Assembly

■ Place each steak on a plate. Pour the roasted vegetable sauce over $1/3$ of each steak and around the plate.

■ Garnish with the grilled onions.

Dessert

Macadamia Lace Cookies

Adapted from a recipe in The Marvelous Macadamia Nut *by Rebecca Buyers (1982, Irena Chalmers Cookbooks, Inc.), these sweets make a fitting addition to a picnic on the Big Island, home to many thousands of acres of macadamia nut trees. Makes 2 dozen cookies.*

Ingredients

8 tablespoons (1 stick) butter
$1/2$ cup light corn syrup
$1/2$ cup light brown sugar, firmly packed
4 teaspoons unsweetened cocoa powder
$1/2$ teaspoon cinnamon
1 cup flour
$1/2$ cup Hawaiian macadamia nuts, chopped into bits

Assembly

■ Preheat the oven to 375 degrees F. Lightly grease 2 cookie sheets.

■ Bring the butter, corn syrup and brown sugar to a boil in a medium saucepan, stirring constantly.

■ Combine the cocoa, cinnamon, flour and macadamia nuts in a small bowl, and gradually stir them into the hot butter mixture.

■ Drop the dough by level tablespoons, about 3 inches apart, onto the cookie sheets.

■ Bake the cookies for 5 to 6 minutes, until they are golden brown and bubbling. Cool them on the sheets for 1 to 2 minutes, then remove them to a wire cooling rack.

Wine Suggestion

Ca'del Solo, Big House Red, California

Big Island Bounty

Amy Ferguson-Ota

Keahole Shrimp, Pohole Ferns with Hichimi (Japanese Pepper Blend)-Roasted

    Garlic Sauce and Tobiko (Flying Fish Roe)

Crispy Thai Chicken

Warm Mango Custard

APPETIZER

Keahole Shrimp, Pohole Ferns with Hichimi-Roasted Garlic Sauce and Tobiko

Amy Ferguson-Ota buys her shrimp from the aquaculture farms of Keahole, because she believes they have the best flavor of any Hawaiian shrimp. Here she poaches the shrimp, but they can also be sautéed or steamed. Serves 4.

Garlic
2 large cloves of garlic
Olive oil to drizzle

Preparation of the Garlic
■ Preheat the oven to 450 degrees F.
■ Peel the garlic and drizzle it with oil. Wrap the garlic in foil, and roast it in the oven for 10 to 15 minutes, or until it is soft, then unwrap.

Crispy Thai Chicken

Hichimi-Roasted Garlic Sauce

1/2 cup fish stock
1 teaspoon finely minced lemongrass
2 large shallots, peeled and minced
1/2 cup Riesling wine
1/4 cup heavy cream
Hichimi (Japanese pepper blend) to taste
1/2 pound unsalted butter, cut into pieces
1/8 cup lemon juice
Salt to taste

Shrimp

4 cups fish stock
1 cup Riesling wine
2 stalks of lemongrass, crushed
16 Keahole shrimp (16-20 size), or any sweet
    shrimp, tail portion peeled and heads intact

Assembly

16 pohole (Hawaii fern) tops, or fiddlehead
    fern tops

Garnish

2 tablespoons tobiko (flying fish roe)
Black sesame seeds for garnish
1 tomato, peeled and diced (optional)
Chopped chives or tarragon (optional)

Preparation of the Hichimi-Roasted Garlic Sauce

- Simmer the fish stock with the lemongrass in a small saucepan for 5 minutes, to infuse the stock.
- Place the garlic, shallots, wine and fish stock in a medium saucepan. Simmer the mixture over medium-high heat for 1 to 2 minutes, until it is reduced to approximately 2 1/2 tablespoons.
- Add the heavy cream and hichimi. Cook the sauce for 1 to 2 minutes, until it has thickened (do not cook too long or it will separate).
- Add the butter to the reduction while whipping with a whisk. Once all the butter is incorporated, adjust the flavor using the lemon, salt and more hichimi.
- Set aside the sauce in a warm spot.

Preparation of the Shrimp

- Combine the fish stock, wine and lemongrass in a large saucepan. Bring the mixture to a boil, and turn off the heat.
- Add the shrimp to the broth, and poach them for 2 to 3 minutes, depending on their size, until they are cooked through.

Assembly

- Arrange the shrimp and ferns on a warm serving platter. Spoon 1 cup of the sauce over the shrimp.
- Garnish the shrimp with the tobiko and sesame seeds. If desired, top the dish with the tomato and chopped herbs.

Crispy Thai Chicken

Chef Ferguson-Ota sometimes replaces the vinegar with lime juice, when she wants to give the sauce a sharper flavor. Serves 6.

Marinade

1/3 cup minced lemongrass

6 cloves garlic, minced

2 tablespoons grated ginger

2 tablespoons fish sauce

1 teaspoon Hawaiian salt, or 1/2 teaspoon kosher salt

1/2 cup rice flour (do not substitute regular flour)

1/2 cup chopped green onion

1/4 cup chopped Chinese parsley

3 tablespoons cornstarch

2 egg whites, slightly beaten

Chicken

3 pounds boneless chicken

Oil for frying

Thai Sauce

1/2 cup red wine vinegar, or lime juice

1/2 cup water

1/4 cup granulated sugar

2 tablespoons fish sauce

1 Hawaiian chili pepper, or 1 tablespoon sambal olek (chili pepper paste)

Assembly

1/2 cup each of Thai basil, Chinese parsley, spearmint, chives, red leaf lettuce, Bibb lettuce or other sweet greens

Garnish

1 cup soft rice noodles (optional)

3/4 cup carrot curls (optional)

1/2 cup chopped peanuts (optional)

Preparation of the Marinade and Chicken

■ Mix all the ingredients for the marinade in a large bowl. Add the chicken, and coat it well with the marinade. Marinate the chicken overnight, if possible.

■ Over low heat, pan-fry the chicken in 1/4 inch of olive oil for 7 to 10 minutes, until it is juicy yet golden brown.

Preparation of the Thai Sauce

■ Mix all the ingredients in a medium bowl. The sauce will keep for 2 weeks in the refrigerator.

Assembly

■ Arrange the greens and herbs in a bed on each plate. Top them with a sprinkling of rice noodles, if desired.

■ Slice the chicken, and fan it out over the greens. If desired, garnish the chicken with the carrot curls and peanuts.

Warm Mango Custard

This dish was originally conceived as an apple custard; when Chef Ferguson-Ota moved to Hawaii, she experimented by adding mangoes, with delicious results. Be sure to use mangoes that are not too ripe, to avoid what she calls "a sticky situation." Serves 12.

Caramel
1 cup granulated sugar
2 tablespoons water

Mangoes
5 or 6 mangoes, or apples, peeled and sliced
2 tablespoons butter

Custard
3/4 cup granulated sugar
3/4 cup plus 2 tablespoons butter
6 eggs
1 cup cream, scalded
1 teaspoon vanilla
1/4 cup Calvados, or Grand Marnier
Dash of salt
Dash each of cinnamon and nutmeg

Topping
3/4 cup flour
1/4 cup granulated sugar
3/4 cup brown sugar

Preparation of the Caramel
■ Bring the sugar and water to a boil in a small saucepan. Cook the mixture over medium heat for 7 to 10 minutes, until it turns golden brown.
■ Line 12 small ramekins (or a 10-inch cake pan) with the caramel.

Preparation of the Mangoes
■ If the mangoes are green and firm, sauté them in the butter for 1 minute. Set the mangoes aside to cool.

Preparation of the Custard
■ Whip the sugar and butter in a medium bowl, and add the eggs, one at a time. Slowly add the cream. Add the vanilla, liqueur, salt, cinnamon and nutmeg to the custard.

Preparation of the Topping
■ Combine all the ingredients in a medium bowl. Set aside.

Assembly

- Preheat the oven to 325 degrees F.
- Place the cooled mangoes on top of the caramel in the molds.
- Pour the custard mixture over them.
- Sprinkle the topping evenly over the custard.
- Place the ramekins in a pyrex dish, and fill the dish with water halfway up the sides of the ramekins, to create a water bath.
- Bake the custard for 50 minutes to 1 hour.
- Test the custard for doneness by inserting a knife in the center. If it comes out clean, the custard is ready.

Wine Suggestion

Orvieto "Amabile," Vaselli, Umbria, Italy, *or*
Yamhill Valley Vineyards Pinot Noir, Oregon

Lanai

Thousands of acres of pineapples once thrived in Lanai's red, iron-rich soil; now, more intimate harvests of spinach, pumpkins, leeks, dryland watercress and lemongrass are the norm. Tourism is fast replacing pineapple growing as Lanai's major industry, and its residents are changing with the times by growing specialty products for the island's two luxury resorts, the Lodge at Koele and the Manele Bay Hotel.

In response, chefs are working closely with farmers as well as fishermen and hunters to create indigenous menus for island visitors. The zucchini grown in small community gardens, for instance, is made into a light oil drizzled on a salad of Lanai greens. A newly caught mahimahi (dolphinfish) is broiled with asparagus and capers and served in a fragrant olive vinaigrette. A deer from the island's large population of wild animals is transformed into grilled Lanai venison salad. As chefs tap Lanai's roots, they come up with specialties such as fresh salmon smoked with aromatic kiawe (mesquite) wood, or Japanese eggplant terrine with toasted goat cheese and crushed plum tomatoes.

Smoked Mahimahi Chowder

Hunter's Luncheon

Darin Schulz

Smoked Mahimahi Chowder

Stirfry of Wild Mushrooms with Puna Goat Cheese

Grilled Lanai Venison Salad

Flourless Red Banana Cake

APPETIZER
Smoked Mahimahi Chowder

In this Darin Schulz signature dish, the smoking of the mahimahi results in a chowder that is rich but not too heavy. Serves 4.

Mahimahi
¹/₃ cup plus 2 teaspoons oil
2 drops Worcestershire sauce
¹/₄ clove minced garlic
Salt and pepper to taste
9 ounces smoked mahimahi (dolphinfish),
   or trout, whitefish or salmon

Chowder
¹/₄ cup olive oil
2 ounces pancetta, chopped
1 leek (white part only), chopped
¹/₄ onion, peeled and chopped
2 ribs celery, chopped
¹/₂ cup flour
2 cups fish stock
1 cup heavy cream
Salt and pepper to taste
Pinch of fresh thyme, chopped
1 large russet potato, boiled until tender,
   peeled and diced

Preparation of the Mahimahi
■ Mix the oil, worcestershire sauce, garlic, salt and pepper in a bowl.
■ Add the mahimahi and marinate for 1 hour. Pat the fish dry.
■ According to your smoker instructions, hot-smoke the mahimahi until just lightly undercooked. Dice into bite-size pieces. Set aside.

Assembly
■ Place the olive oil in a large pot over medium heat. Add the pancetta and sauté for 4 to 5 minutes. Add the leek, onion and celery. Sauté an additional 4 to 5 minutes.
■ Add the flour and cook for 2 minutes. Add the stock slowly and bring to a boil. Let the mixture simmer for 10 minutes.
■ Add the cream and reduce the mixture to preferred soup consistency, approximately 4 to 5 minutes. Season with the salt, pepper and thyme. Add the mahimahi and potato.
■ Serve in bowls.

Stirfry of Wild Mushrooms with Puna Goat Cheese

The term "wild mushrooms" refers not to mushrooms that are picked in the wild, but to exotic mushrooms that are cultivated on farms. Each variety of wild mushroom has its own distinctive taste; "oysters" are the subtlest in flavor, for instance, while morels and chanterelles are earthy and "lobsters" are sweet. Serves 4.

Balsamic Vinaigrette
Pinch of minced garlic (less than 1/2 clove)
1/2 teaspoon Dijon mustard
2 tablespoons balsamic vinegar
1/4 cup olive oil
Salt to taste
Pinch of freshly ground pepper

Mushroom Mixture
1 tablespoon vegetable oil
1/2 teaspoon minced shallots
6 cups wild mushrooms, sliced or quartered
2 tablespoons dry white wine
Pinch of a mixture of chopped chives, chervil, marjoram and parsley
Salt and pepper to taste

Goat Cheese Croutons
1/4 pound Puna goat cheese, or your local goat cheese
1/4 cup tablespoon flour
1 egg, beaten
1 cup panko (Japanese shaved bread crumbs) or any unseasoned fresh bread crumbs
Oil for frying

Salad
10 cups mesclun greens (mixed baby lettuces)

Preparation of the Balsamic Vinaigrette
■ Place the garlic and mustard in a medium stainless-steel bowl, add the vinegar, and whisk. Slowly add the olive oil while continuing to whisk, until the oil is incorporated. Season with the salt and pepper.

Preparation of the Mushroom Mixture
■ Place the oil in a hot wok or sauté pan and add the shallots and mushrooms. Stirfry for 15 seconds.
■ Add the wine and reduce the mixture for about 30 seconds, until it is dry. Add the herbs and season the mixture with salt and pepper. Remove the pan from the heat and set aside.

Preparation of the Goat Cheese Croutons
■ Slice the goat cheese into 4 equal parts. Place one piece of the cheese in the flour and lightly coat all sides. Dip the cheese in the egg, then in the crumbs, and pack it well. Repeat the process with the remaining cheese, until all the pieces are well breaded.
■ Heat 1/4 inch of oil in a sauté pan. Fry the pieces of cheese in hot oil until they turn golden brown on all sides. Remove the cheese pieces from the oil and place them on a towel to absorb any excess oil. Set aside.

Assembly
■ Place the greens in a bowl, add the vinaigrette and toss lightly. Arrange the tossed greens on plates.
■ Place the stirfried mushrooms on top of the greens.
■ Place the goat cheese croutons on the plates and serve.

Grilled Lanai Venison Salad

With a deer population twice that of its human residents, Lanai is a popular island for hunters. Due to the low fat content of venison, this dish is best when prepared medium-rare. Serves 2.

Beans

16 baby green beans

Vegetable Vinaigrette

3 tablespoons fresh carrot juice
1 tablespoon fresh fennel juice
1 tablespoon fresh zucchini juice (using the outside of the zucchini only)
1 tablespoon fresh beet juice
1 tablespoon rice wine vinegar
2 tablespoons grapeseed oil
2 drops kiawe (mesquite) honey or any clover honey

Oils for Garnish

1 tablespoon carrot juice
¼ cup grapeseed oil
1 tablespoon fennel juice
1 tablespoon zucchini juice
1 tablespoon beet juice

Venison

6 ounces trimmed venison loin, or chicken, shrimp or steak
Salt and pepper to taste

Preparation of the Beans

■ In 1 quart of salted boiling water, blanch the green beans for 1 minute, then place them in ice water to shock them.

Preparation of the Vegetable Vinaigrette

■ Combine all the juice in a blender with the vinegar. While the machine is running, slowly pour in the oil, then add the honey. Season to taste with the salt and pepper. Set aside.

Preparation of the Oils for Garnish

■ (Note: Each oil must be made separately in a blender, one at a time, and each oil may be made in advance and stored in the refrigerator for up to 5 days.)
■ Place the carrot juice in blender. While the machine is running, slowly add 1 tablespoon of the grapeseed oil. Blend 10 to 20 seconds until the oil is emulsified with the juice. Place the oil in a plastic squeeze bottle.
■ Repeat this process with the fennel, zucchini and beet juices, placing each oil in a separate squeeze bottle.

Assembly

■ Season the venison loin with the salt and pepper and place it on a grill. Cook the meat to your desired doneness.
■ Place the greens and beans in a stainless-steel bowl. Add the vinaigrette and toss the mixture.
■ Place the greens in the center of a plate. Arrange the beans around the lettuce.
■ Slice the venison and shingle the slices on top of the greens.
■ To garnish, drizzle individual oils on the plate around the salad. Serve immediately.

Flourless Red Banana Cake

The red banana is a high-fiber baking fruit that is meatier and stronger in flavor than the more common yellow banana. Serves 2.

Berry Sauce
2 pints fresh berries (raspberries, blackberries or whatever is in season)
Juice of 2 lemons
Sugar to taste

Cake
8 egg yolks
¾ cup sugar
4 red bananas, or apple bananas, plus banana slices for garnish
¼ cup amaretto liqueur
¼ cup crème de cacao liqueur
8 egg whites

Preparation of the Berry Sauce
- Puree the berries in a blender 15-20 seconds, until they are very smooth.
- Strain the mixture through a fine sieve to remove the seeds.
- Stir in the lemon juice and sugar.
- Refrigerate the mixture, tightly covered, until serving time.

Preparation of the Cake
- Preheat the oven to 350 degrees F.
- Grease and sugar a 3x6-inch loaf pan.
- Combine the yolks, sugar, bananas, amaretto and crème de cacao in a food processor and puree the mixture about 15 seconds, until it is smooth.
- Place the egg whites in a large stainless-steel bowl, and whip them to stiff peaks.
- Fold the whites carefully into the pureed mixture. Immediately pour the mixture into the pan.
- Bake the cake at 350 degrees until it is golden brown.
- Allow the cake to cool and fall.

Assembly
- Garnish the top of the cake with the additional banana slices and serve it with the berry sauce.

Wine Suggestion
Domaine de la Gautière Red, Provence, France

Mediterranean Style

Philippe Padovani

Fresh Kona Oysters with Hawaiian Mignonette

Kahuku Prawn, Papaya and Mesclun Salad with

    Sweet-and-Sour Vinaigrette

Wok-Fried Moana (Goatfish) with Tabbouleh Salad, Tomato and Niçoise

    Olives Vinaigrette

Exotic Fresh Fruits with Chocolate Lilikoi Sabayon

APPETIZER
Fresh Kona Oysters with Hawaiian Mignonette

For this dish, Padovani makes a mignonette in honor of his native France, but includes ogo, ginger and mirin in response to the Asian cultures of his adopted home. Serves 4.

Hawaiian Mignonette

¼ cup finely chopped shallots

⅓ cup finely chopped pickled ginger, or fresh ginger

¼ cup finely chopped red ogo (seaweed), or dry seaweed

2 tablespoons finely chopped cilantro

½ cup rice wine vinegar

½ cup mirin (sweet Japanese rice wine, available in Asian markets)

2 tablespoons lemon juice

Salt and white pepper to taste

Preparation of the Hawaiian Mignonette

■ Mix the shallots, ginger, ogo, cilantro, vinegar, mirin and lemon juice in a bowl with a whisk.

■ Season the mixture with salt and pepper, and set aside.

Assembly

■ Chill 4 dinner plates and line the bottom of each with crushed ice or rock salt.

Fresh Kona Oysters with Hawaiian Mignonette

Oysters

24 Kona oysters, or Pacific oysters, shucked without the nerve

Crushed ice or rock salt

Garnish

Whole ogo or parsley

Prawns

2 pounds Kahuku prawns, or red shrimp

Salt and pepper to taste

2 tablespoons sesame oil

Sweet-and-Sour Vinaigrette

3 tablespoons lime juice

2 tablespoons sugar

2 tablespoons fish sauce

1/2 teaspoon Chinese chili sauce, or Thai chili sauce

2 teaspoons green onions, minced

1 tablespoon minced cilantro

Papaya/Pepper/Cucumber

1 Puna papaya, or any ripe papaya

1 small red bell pepper

1/2 Japanese cucumber

Salad

10 cups mesclun greens (mixed baby lettuces)

1/2 cup Hawaiian macadamia nuts, roasted and cut in half

1 small bunch cilantro leaves

- Arrange 6 oysters on each plate, then pour 1 tablespoon of the mignonette over every oyster.
- Decorate the center of each dish with a sprig of ogo.
- Serve chilled, immediately.

SALAD

Kahuku Prawn, Papaya and Mesclun Salad with Sweet-and-Sour Vinaigrette

Padovani looks to the North Shore of Oahu—specifically, the town of Kahuku—for his prawns, which are grown in freshwater ponds and which have a sweet, fresh, rich flavor. Serves 4.

Preparation of the Prawns

- Clean only the tails of the prawns; season the prawns with salt and pepper.
- Heat the sesame oil in a non-stick pan. Pan-fry the prawns in the oil, cooking them 2 to 4 minutes until their flesh turns coral pink. Set aside.

Preparation of the Sweet-and-Sour Vinaigrette

- Combine the lime juice, sugar, fish sauce, chili sauce, green onions and cilantro in a jar and shake vigorously. Set aside.

Preparation of the Papaya/Pepper/Cucumber:

- Peel and seed the papaya. Cut it into 1/2-inch cubes.
- Stem and seed the pepper. Cut it into 1/2-inch triangles.
- Split the cucumber in half lengthwise and scrape out the seeds. Cut it into long 1/4-inch strips, then place the strips together and cut them into 1/2-inch cubes.
- Set aside all of these ingredients.

Assembly

- Toss the mesclun greens with the vinaigrette. Place equal amounts of the greens on 4 plates.
- Arrange the papaya, prawns, red bell pepper, cucumber, macadamia nuts and cilantro leaves to finish the dish.
- Serve immediately.

Wok-Fried Moana with Tabbouleh Salad, Tomato and Niçoise Olives Vinaigrette

With its arcaded loggias and sloping roofs, The Manele Bay Hotel has a decidedly Mediterranean feeling. Padovani plays off that mood by adding tabbouleh and Niçoise olives to this recipe. Serves 4.

Moana

2 pounds whole moana, or catfish, scaled and cleaned
1/4 cup virgin olive oil
1 sprig fresh thyme
2 cloves garlic, peeled
Oil for frying
Salt and pepper to taste
1/2 cup cornstarch

Tabbouleh

1 cup cooked couscous
1/4 cup chicken stock
1/4 cup virgin olive oil
2 tablespoons lemon juice
1/4 cup sherry vinegar
2 tablespoons capers
1/4 cup fresh corn
2 tablespoons finely chopped chives
2 tablespoons finely chopped chervil
2 tablespoons finely chopped parsley
Salt and white pepper to taste

Tomato and Niçoise Olive Vinaigrette

1 cup (2 medium) diced tomatoes
2 teaspoons Pommery mustard
2 tablespoons sherry vinegar
2 tablespoons finely chopped shallots
1 teaspoon capers
1/4 cup Niçoise olives
1/2 cup olive oil
2 tablespoons finely chopped chives
Salt and pepper to taste

Preparation of the Moana

■ Make shallow cuts on the surface of the moana. Marinate the fish in the oil with thyme and garlic for 20 minutes, then pat it dry.
■ Heat the wok and add the oil for frying. Season the moana with the salt and pepper and coat it with the cornstarch.
■ Deep-fry the moana for approximately 10 to 12 minutes or until it is golden brown.

Preparation of the Tabbouleh

■ In a salad bowl, mix the couscous, stock, oil, lemon juice, vinegar, capers, corn and herbs. Season with the salt and pepper, then mix the ingredients thoroughly.
■ Chill in the refrigerator for at least 3 hours.

Preparation of the Tomatoes for the Vinaigrette

■ Blanch the tomatoes. Cut finely across the top of the tomatoes, just deep enough to cut the skin.
■ Drop the tomatoes into rapidly boiling water. After 30 seconds, drain and run them under cold water until the tomatoes are cool enough to handle. Peel the skin off.
■ Quarter the tomatoes and remove the pulp and seeds, leaving petals of tomato flesh. Cut them in half.

Preparation of the Tomato and Niçoise Olive Vinaigrette

■ In a medium bowl, mix the mustard and vinegar well. Add the tomatoes and remaining ingredients.

Assembly

■ Spread the tabbouleh to the shape of an oval plate and to the size of the fish being served.
■ Place the moana on the plate of tabbouleh. Pour the vinaigrette over the fish.

Exotic Fresh Fruits with Chocolate Lilikoi Sabayon

Fashioned from cocoa beans grown on the Big Island, Hawaiian Vintage Chocolate has found a major fan in Padovani. Here, he successfully pairs the chocolate's strong flavor with the fresh fruits of Lanai. Serves 4.

Fruit
2 papayas
2 mangoes
12 strawberries

Sabayon
2 ounces Hawaiian Vintage Chocolate, or any fine chocolate
6 egg yolks
¼ cup sugar
¼ cup water
¼ cup fresh lilikoi (passion fruit), or passion fruit juice

Garnish
4 sprigs of fresh mint

Preparation of the Fruit
- Peel the papaya and prepare it into melon balls.
- Peel and seed the mango and slice it finely lengthwise.
- Clean the strawberries, remove their stems and slice them.

Preparation of the Chocolate
- Melt the chocolate in a medium bowl over a double boiler. Remove the chocolate from the heat.

Preparation of the Sabayon
- In a large bowl, cream the egg yolks and sugar well, but do not beat them.
- Add the water.
- Place the bowl in a water bath, taking great care that the bottom of the bowl containing the egg and sugar mixture does not touch the hot bottom of the pan beneath.
- Pour in the lilikoi, stirring continuously. The water in the bath should not come to a boil again, but it should be kept just below the simmering point.
- Beat the mixture energetically with a whisk until it froths and doubles in volume (when lifted with a spoon, it should flow back down to the bowl like a thick ribbon).
- Combine the sabayon with the melted chocolate.

Assembly

- On a 12-inch plate, arrange ¼ of the mango slices into a triangle, leaving the center empty. Add ¼ of the strawberries inside the triangle.
- Add ¼ of the papaya balls in the center. Repeat for the rest of the plates.
- Pour ¼ cup sabayon around the sides of each plate, letting it touch the fruit slightly.
- Garnish with mint.

Wine Suggestions

Zenato, Pinot Griglio, Veneto, Italy, *or*
Coldridge, Semillon/Chardonnay, Victoria, Australia, *or*
Bonny Doon, Vin Gris de Cigare Rosé, California

Hot Cuisine

Chefs in warm climates tend to showcase foods with flavors derived from herbs and spices rather than butter and cream. For instance, Roy Yamaguchi's charmoula-style opakapaka combines three spices in different degrees of intensity: cayenne, a red-hot chili ground to a fine texture; paprika, a mild, sweet powder from the fruit of several peppers; and cumin, a pungent, earthy spice.

The foods of sunny locales around the world find an appropriate forum in Hawaii, at three annual food-and-wine events. In May, at the Ritz-Carlton Mauna Lani's Big Island Bounty, chefs introduce guests to local farmers and other food producers. The chefs showcase those products at gourmet sit-down dinners with dishes such as nori (dried seaweed) fettuccine and opihi (limpets) with garlic-chili butter sauce.

July brings Cuisines of the Sun, hosted by the Mauna Lani Bay Hotel & Bungalows, on the Big Island. At this festive food fair, guests watch chefs create Sunbelt specialties such as grilled Florida swordfish in mango Scotch barbecue sauce. They discuss the complex flavors of Balinese beef satay with peanut sauce and sambal matah (raw shallots and lemongrass). And they might even learn how to make mai tais at a tropical drink seminar.

At the venerable Kapalua Wine Symposium, also held in July, gourmets gather at a seaside Maui resort for lively discussions on the pairing of food and wine. Their conversations culminate in elaborate evening feasts; for instance, chilled green tomato soup is paired with a Chalk Hill chardonnay, while rack of lamb in a spicy red Thai curry sauce finds its match in a Rodney Strong pinot noir.

Crispy Calamari Salad with Lemon Olive Oil, Soy Vinaigrette and Shaved Parmesan

Hot Summer Nights

Roy Yamaguchi

Full Moons of Lamb with Capers, Olives, Tomatoes and Ginger

Crispy Calamari Salad with Lemon Olive Oil, Soy Vinaigrette and

    Shaved Parmesan

Opakapaka Charmoula-Style with Grilled Vegetable Gratin

Guava Granita

APPETIZER

Full Moons of Lamb with Capers, Olives, Tomatoes and Ginger

Leftover lamb can be used in this dish; otherwise, first sauté or grill a leg of lamb until it is medium-rare. Serves 4.

Lamb
1/2 pound lamb

Filling
1 teaspoon minced garlic
2 tablespoons olive oil
7 cups spinach
1/2 cup goat cheese
1/2 cup ricotta cheese
Salt and pepper to taste

Preparation of the Lamb
■ Precook the lamb to medium-rare and dice it into 1/4-inch squares.

Preparation of the Filling
■ In a skillet over medium heat, sauté the garlic in the oil for about 10 seconds. Add the spinach and sauté the mixture for 30 seconds or until the spinach is fully cooked.
■ Remove the spinach from the pan, squeeze out the excess liquid and mix it in a medium bowl with the goat cheese, ricotta and cooked lamb. Season the mixture with salt and pepper, and set it aside.

102

Cornstarch Mixture

2 tablespoons cornstarch
2 tablespoons water
1 teaspoon oil

Full Moons

32 gyoza (pot sticker) wrappers, or wonton
    wrappers

Sauce

2 cloves garlic, minced
1 teaspoon minced ginger
½ cup olive oil
¼ cup julienned leeks
1½ tablespoons capers
1 tomato, peeled, seeded and diced
16 pitted Niçoise olives
Salt and pepper to taste

Salad Mixture

5 cups baby lettuce leaves

Preparation of the Cornstarch Mixture

■ In a small bowl, dissolve the cornstarch in the water. Add the oil and mix it in well.

Assembly of the Full Moons

■ Place 16 of the gyoza wrappers on a flat surface. Place 2 tablespoons of the filling in the middle of each wrapper.
■ To seal the full moons, brush the cornstarch water around the edge of the wrapper and cover it with another gyoza wrapper, which results in a round package.
■ Place the full moons in boiling water, and cook for 2 minutes.

Preparation of the Sauce

■ In a skillet over moderate heat, sauté the garlic and ginger in the oil for 10 seconds.
■ Add the leeks, capers, tomatoes and olives. Sauté the mixture for 1 minute. Season the sauce with the salt and pepper, and set it aside.

Assembly

■ Place 4 full moons in each soup bowl. Pour ¼ of the sauce over the full moons in each bowl and top the dish with equal amounts of the salad mixture.

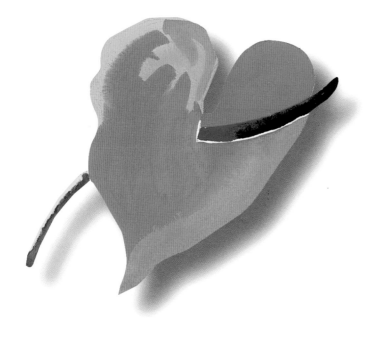

Crispy Calamari Salad with Lemon Olive Oil, Soy Vinaigrette and Shaved Parmesan

If calamari is not available, Chef Yamaguchi recommends shrimp as a substitute. Serves 4.

Calamari

½ cup flour

1 tablespoon hichimi (Japanese pepper blend), or cayenne

¾ pound calamari, cut into rings, or whole shrimp

1 quart frying oil

Salad

2½ cups baby romaine, or your favorite lettuce

2½ cups radicchio, or your favorite lettuce

2½ cups mizuna, or your favorite lettuce

Dressing

1 tablespoon minced garlic

1 tablespoon minced ginger

1 tablespoon minced lemongrass

¼ cup olive oil

1 tablespoon soy sauce

1 tablespoon lemon juice

Garnish

¼ cup shaved parmesan cheese

Preparation of the Calamari

- Combine the flour and hichimi, then dredge the calamari in the flour mixture.
- Over high heat, deep-fry the calamari in the oil until it is crispy, about 45 seconds. Remove and place the calamari on a paper towel.

Preparation of the Salad

- Toss all the ingredients in a medium bowl and set aside.

Preparation of the Dressing

- In a skillet over medium heat, sauté the garlic, ginger and lemongrass in the oil for 15 seconds. Add the soy sauce and lemon juice and pour the mixture over the salad, then toss it.

Assembly

- Place the salad on a plate and top it with the calamari.
- Garnish the salad with the parmesan.

ENTREE
Opakapaka Charmoula-Style with Grilled Vegetable Gratin

"Charmoula" refers to a spicy Moroccan marinade that Yamaguchi favors when working with opakapaka. Serves 4.

Charmoula and Fish
$\frac{1}{2}$ cup olive oil
$\frac{1}{4}$ cup lemon juice
$\frac{1}{4}$ cup chopped parsley
$\frac{1}{4}$ cup chopped cilantro
3 cloves garlic, minced
$\frac{1}{2}$ tablespoon paprika
1 teaspoon ground cumin
$\frac{1}{4}$ teaspoon cayenne
Salt and pepper to taste
4 (8-ounce) opakapaka (pink snapper) fillets, or any snapper

Vegetable Gratin
$\frac{1}{2}$ tablespoon minced garlic
$\frac{1}{2}$ teaspoon olive oil
2 Japanese eggplants, sliced lengthwise
2 zucchini, sliced lengthwise
1 tomato, sliced in quarters
1 Maui onion, or any sweet onion, sliced in quarters
$\frac{1}{4}$ pound mozzarella cheese, thinly sliced

Preparation of the Charmoula and Fish
- To make the charmoula, combine all of the ingredients except the fish in a large bowl. Set aside $\frac{1}{4}$ cup of the charmoula for the garnish.
- Marinate the fish in the remaining charmoula for 3 hours.

Preparation of the Vegetable Gratin
- Preheat the oven to 350 degrees F.
- Mix the garlic and olive oil in a medium bowl. Marinate the eggplant, zucchini, tomatoes and onions in the garlic/oil mixture for 1 minute.
- Grill the marinated vegetables for about $1\frac{1}{2}$ minutes per side. Place the slices of eggplant, zucchini, tomato and Maui onion in 4 stacks, each containing slices of all the vegetables. Top off each stack with the sliced mozzarella cheese.
- Bake the stacks for 2 minutes until the cheese has melted. The stacks can also be broiled for 30 to 45 seconds.

Assembly
- Grill the fish for $1\frac{1}{2}$ minutes on each side, or until desired doneness.
- Arrange the vegetables on a plate with the grilled fish, and garnish the fish with the reserved charmoula.

Guava Granita

An Italian-derived dish similar to an ice, granita is often used as an intermezzo between courses. If guava juice is not available, orange, pineapple or grapefruit juice work equally well in this recipe. Serves 8.

Ingredients
Grated zest of 1 lemon
Grated zest of 1 orange
1½ cups guava juice
1 cup granulated sugar
1½ cups champagne

Assembly
■ In a small saucepan filled with water, boil the lemon and orange zest for 1 minute. Strain the mixture and place the zest in a bowl.

■ Bring the guava juice and sugar to a boil in a medium saucepan. Dissolve the sugar and add it to the zest. Stir in the champagne.

■ Place the mixture in a 10-inch square, 2-inch deep pan and place it in the freezer.

■ Mix the granita with a fork every 30 minutes once it starts to crystallize, for about 2 to 2½ hours, until it has reached a shave-ice, or snow-cone consistency.

Wine suggestion
Gavi La Rocca, Piedmont, Italy, *or*
Mitchelton, Marsanne, Australia

French Tropical

Philippe Padovani

Shrimp Salad with Mango and Grapes, Sweet-and-Sour Coconut Vinaigrette

Beggars' Purses and Dungeness Crab with Avocado Fish Roe Sauce

Medallions of Lobster with a Nage of Shiitake

Hawaiian Vintage Chocolate Macadamia Nut Lava Rocks

APPETIZER
Shrimp Salad with Mango and Grapes, Sweet-and-Sour Coconut Vinaigrette

Padovani buys his mango from the Big Island and Oahu. Whenever possible, he uses the Haden variety because of its juicy, flavorful flesh, but Pirie and Gouveia varieties are also highly prized. Serves 4.

Sweet-and-Sour Coconut Vinaigrette
½ cup coconut milk
2 tablespoons oriental chili paste
1 tablespoon palm sugar (Thai sugar paste), or brown sugar
2 tablespoons fish sauce
2 tablespoons lime juice

Garlic and Shallots
2 tablespoons sliced garlic
2 tablespoons sliced shallots
¼ cup oil

Preparation of the Sweet-and-Sour Coconut Vinaigrette
■ Bring the coconut milk to a boil in a medium saucepan. Add the chili paste, palm sugar, fish sauce and lime juice. Stir the mixture for 2 to 3 minutes until the ingredients have dissolved and the vinaigrette is well-mixed and fragrant. Set it aside to cool.

Preparation of the Garlic and Shallots
■ Sauté the garlic and shallots in the oil for 2 to 3 minutes, until they are crispy. Remove them from the oil and set them aside to dry.

107

Shrimp Salad

4 large lettuce leaves

1 Haden mango, or any ripe mango, sliced into orange wedge-size segments

4 cups halved green and black grapes

1 red chili, finely diced

32 small shrimp, shelled and deveined

Garnish

¼ cup whole cilantro leaves

Assembly of the Shrimp Salad

- Create 4 cups out of the lettuce leaves.
- In a mixing bowl, add the mango, grapes, chili and shrimp to the coconut vinaigrette. Mix the ingredients well, then add the garlic, shallots and cilantro leaves. Taste the mixture and adjust the seasonings if needed.
- Serve the salad immediately in the lettuce cups.

SIDE DISH

Beggars' Purses and Dungeness Crab with Avocado Fish Roe Sauce

Part of the nouvelle cuisine craze that started in France in the mid-1970s, beggars' purses are like little stuffed crepes. Chef Padovani updates the recipe with rich crabmeat and a sauce of smooth avocado and crunchy fish roe. Serves 4.

Crab

½ cup rock salt to taste

1½ to 2 pounds live Dungeness crab, or any shellfish, enough to yield 1½ cups of meat

Crepe Batter

1¼ cups flour

2 eggs

¾ cup milk

¾ cup chicken stock

Salt to taste

1 teaspoon melted butter

Preparation of the Crab

- In a large pot, season a gallon of water with the rock salt and bring it to a boil; plunge the live crab into the water.
- When the water returns to a boil, cook the crab for approximately 12 minutes.
- After the crab is cooked, cool it in ice water, then crack and clean it. This should yield about 1½ cups of meat. Set the meat aside.

Preparation of the Crepe Batter

- In a large bowl, combine the flour, eggs, milk, chicken stock and salt. Mix the ingredients until they are smooth.
- Strain the batter through a fine sieve, then stir in the melted butter. Set the mixture aside for 1 hour before cooking the crepes. Brush just enough oil on a 6-inch non-stick pan to create a shine.
- Pour approximately 2 tablespoons of batter into the pan, enough to make a thin, 6-inch-wide crepe. Fry the crepe for 2 to 3 minutes and set it aside on a plate, covered, at room temperature.

Avocado Fish Roe Sauce
½ avocado
Juice of ½ lemon
2 tablespoons chicken stock
½ cup crème fraîche, or sour cream
Salt and pepper to taste
3 tablespoons fish roe

Garnish
12 chives
1 tablespoon fish roe
1 tablespoon beluga caviar

■ Repeat this process to make 12 crepes.

Preparation of the Avocado Fish Roe Sauce
■ Mash the avocado to a puree, then add the lemon juice. With a whisk, mix in the chicken stock and crème fraîche. Season the mixture with salt and pepper, then strain it through a fine mesh. Add the fish roe to the mixture and set it aside.

Preparation of the Garnish
■ Blanch the chives by plunging them in hot water for 5 seconds, then remove and ice them. The chives should be soft but still green.

Assembly of the Beggars' Purses
■ In a large mixing bowl, add the crab and half of the avocado sauce and mix well. Season the mixture to taste.
■ Place a tablespoon of the crab mixture in the center of each crepe. Fold each crepe upward as if to make a bag. Using the chives like string, tie each crepe closed.
■ On each plate, create a triangle design using 3 tablespoons of the remaining avocado sauce. Place three crepes in the center of each triangle and decorate the crepes with the fish roe and caviar. Serve chilled.

ENTREE
Medallions of Lobster with a Nage of Shiitake

In French cooking, nage means broth, which is the basis of the following dish. This can also be served as an appetizer. Serves 4.

Lobsters
2 (1¼ pounds each) live lobsters

Lemongrass Stock
1 cup water
2 cups white wine
¼ cup finely chopped carrots
¼ cup finely chopped onions
¼ cup finely chopped shallots
¼ cup finely chopped celery leaves
1 stalk lemongrass, finely chopped
2 whole cloves garlic, peeled
2 cloves
1 bouquet garni of bay leaves and parsley
Juice of ½ lemon
1 tablespoon of rock salt
Dash of white pepper
Pinch of cayenne pepper

Nage of Shiitake
1 cup butter
4 cups finely sliced fresh shiitake mushrooms, or
  morels
Juice of ½ lemon
Salt and pepper to taste

Garnish
2 sprigs mint, finely julienned

Preparation of the Lobsters
■ Cook the lobsters in boiling salted water for 7 to 8 minutes. Remove the lobsters from the water and let them cool.
■ Remove the lobster heads, peel the tails and break the claws, then remove the meat. Slice each tail into 4 pieces and set aside.

Preparation of the Lemongrass Stock
■ Bring the water and wine to a boil. Add the chopped vegetables, aromatic herbs and lemon juice. Continue to boil the mixture for another 30 minutes. After 15 minutes, add the salt and pepper. Set the clear stock aside and discard the ingredients.

Preparation of the Nage of Shiitake
■ Heat 2 cups of the lemongrass stock in a large saucepan over high heat. Whip the butter into the stock with a whisk, then add the mushrooms and lemon juice. Bring the mixture to a boil for 2 minutes. Season it to taste.

Assembly
■ Preheat 4 soup plates.
■ Pour some of the nage of shiitake into each soup plate. Divide the medallions of lobster into 4 equal portions and arrange them on the nage.
■ Sprinkle with fresh mint and serve immediately.

DESSERT

Hawaiian Vintage Chocolate Macadamia Nut Lava Rocks

When working with chocolate, room temperature can greatly affect the results. For this recipe, Padovani advises a room temperature of 75 to 80 degrees. Makes 6 dozen candies.

Macadamia Nuts
½ cup sugar
1 tablespoon water
3½ cups Hawaiian macadamia nuts, diced and
 roasted
1 tablespoon butter

Chocolate
9½ ounces Hawaiian Vintage dark chocolate
 pistoles (flat, quarter-size discs), or any fine
 semisweet chocolate

Preparation of the Macadamia Nuts
■ Cook the sugar and water in a small saucepan until the mixture is lightly boiling (234 degrees F). Immediately pour the macadamia nuts into the syrup and mix well.
■ Cook the nut mixture slowly for 5 to 6 minutes, until it becomes a light caramel. Add the butter and mix well.
■ Place the macadamia nuts on a sheet pan and set them aside.

Preparation of the Chocolate

■ Melt ⅔ of the chocolate in a double boiler at 113–122 degrees F, but not over an open flame. Pour the remaining ⅓ of the pistoles into the bowl. Stir the chocolate carefully with a spatula until it is completely melted. Reheat the chocolate quickly for a greater fluidity, and use it at 88–90 degrees F.

To Finish the Lava Rocks

■ Pour the macadamia nuts into the melted chocolate. Mix them well with a spatula. Spoon the mixture by teaspoonfuls onto parchment paper and let it cool. Serve the candy when it has hardened, which takes 5 minutes in a 75- to 80-degree room.

Wine Suggestion

Clos Nicrosi, Corsica, France, *or*
Logan Chardonnay, Monterey, California

Molokai

In unselfish fashion, Molokai not only produces but it provides. A predominantly flat and rural island with two small mountains, it acts as Hawaii's breadbasket, from which spring many of the fruits, vegetables and seafood products that serve as the foundation of the new cuisine of Hawaii.

One Molokai family grows the vine-ripened tomatoes that turn up in a Maui hotel salad with goat cheese and eggplant. Another specializes in the potatoes and baby corn that intermingle in a Kauai chef's sweet chowder. Still others work with taro, a starchy edible tuber which can be julienned and deep-fried as a garnish for Roy Yamaguchi's grilled chicken with black bean-mango salsa.

Molokai farmers gather and sell mangoes and bananas that contribute ultra-fresh local flavors to a tropical fruit compote. The fishermen of the island catch opakapaka (pink snapper), which can be baked with coconut milk and served with julienned bamboo. From dawn to dusk, men work the island's centuries-old shoreline fish ponds, within whose rock walls are grown ogo (seaweed) for ahi poke (marinated tuna).

This laid-back island may boast fertile soil and seas, but its restaurants are anything but gourmet. The unpretentious lifestyle of Molokai's people is reflected in the honey-dipped chicken served at a casual hotel restaurant, or the teriyaki beef plate lunches sold every day from a funky carryout.

Seafood Half-Moons with a Watercress Ginger Nage

Tastes of Molokai

Roy Yamaguchi

Seafood Half-Moons with a Watercress Ginger Nage

Spicy Thai Beef Salad in a Sesame Seed Mint Vinaigrette

Grilled Chicken with Black Bean Mango Salsa and Crispy Taro

Tropical Fruit Compote

APPETIZER

Seafood Half-Moons with a Watercress Ginger Nage

When selecting ginger, a knobby brown root with a pungent flavor, make sure that it is smooth, not withered. After slicing off the amount you need, keep the rest of the root in the refrigerator for several weeks by wrapping it tightly with plastic wrap. Serves 4.

Cornstarch Mixture
2 tablespoons water
2 tablespoons cornstarch
1 teaspoon olive oil

Seafood Half-Moons
½ pound peeled, raw shrimp
½ pound raw scallops
6 tablespoons heavy cream
1 egg
1 tablespoon minced basil
¼ teaspoon minced garlic
¼ teaspoon minced tarragon
Salt and pepper to taste
16 gyoza (pot sticker) wrappers, or wonton wrappers

Preparation of the Cornstarch Mixture
■ Mix the water with the cornstarch in a small bowl until it dissolves. Stir in the oil and set the bowl aside.

Preparation of the Seafood Half-Moons
■ Puree the shrimp and scallops in a food processor for 15 to 30 seconds until they become a coarse grind.
■ Turn off the food processor and add the cream, egg, basil, garlic and tarragon to the seafood. Puree the mixture for 30 to 45 seconds until all the ingredients are incorporated.
■ Season the mixture with the salt and pepper, then transfer it to a medium bowl.
■ Fill each wrapper with 1 tablespoon of filling, folding it in half to make a half-moon, and seal the edges with the cornstarch mixture.

Sauce

1 tablespoon minced ginger
½ cup white wine (chablis or chardonnay)
2 tablespoons white vinegar
1 large shallot, minced
2 tablespoons heavy cream
1 cup unsalted butter
Salt and pepper to taste

Watercress

1 cup watercress leaves
1 quart hot water

Preparation of the Sauce

■ Combine the ginger, wine, vinegar and shallots in a saucepan over medium heat.
■ Reduce the mixture for 10 to 15 minutes, to 2 tablespoons, until it reaches a syrupy consistency.
■ Add the cream and cook the mixture for 45 seconds to 1 minute, until it has reduced by ⅓, to 2 tablespoons. Slowly whisk in the butter.
■ Season the mixture with the salt and pepper, strain and set it aside.

Preparation of the Watercress

■ Blanch the watercress leaves in hot water for 15 seconds, and drain them. Squeeze the water out of the leaves and mince them fine.
■ Add the leaves to the sauce.

Assembly

■ Place the half-moons in boiling water and cook them for about 2 minutes.
■ Place 4 half-moons in each soup bowl and spoon ¼ cup of sauce over each serving.

Salad Mix

½ cup julienned seedless cucumber, skin on
½ cup bean sprouts
20 mint leaves
20 basil leaves
½ cup watercress leaves
2½ cups mizuna
2½ cups radicchio

SALAD

Spicy Thai Beef Salad in a Sesame Seed Mint Vinaigrette

Your preferred salad mix may be substituted for the watercress, mizuna and radicchio. Serves 4.

Preparation of the Salad Mix

■ Mix all of the ingredients in a medium bowl. Set aside.

Preparation of the Beef and Dressing

■ Cut the steak into 4-ounce portions, or into 1-by-2-inch strips.
■ Salt and pepper the steak and sauté it in the olive oil over medium-high heat for 1½ minutes per side, until it is medium-rare.

Thai Beef and Dressing

1 pound New York steak
Salt and pepper to season
6 tablespoons olive oil
1 teaspoon minced lemongrass
1 teaspoon minced shallots
2 cloves garlic, minced
1 teaspoon minced kaffir lime leaves
1/2 teaspoon sugar
1 tablespoon soy sauce
1/2 tablespoon fish sauce
1 tablespoon lemon juice

- In the pan used to cook the beef, add the lemongrass, shallots, garlic and lime leaves and lightly brown them for about 10 seconds.
- Add the sugar, soy sauce, fish sauce and lemon juice.
- Remove the steak and set it aside.

Assembly

- Pour the dressing over the salad and mix them together.
- Divide the salad equally among 4 plates and arrange the sliced beef on top of the salad.

Grilled Chicken with Black Bean Mango Salsa and Crispy Taro

Taro has long been associated with the Hawaiian diet, primarily as a source of the nutritious paste called poi. But as this recipe demonstrates, chefs are dreaming up creative new uses for the tuber. Serves 4.

Black Bean Mango Salsa

1/2 cup black beans
4 cups water
1/2 cup diced onions
2 tablespoons olive oil
1/8 teaspoon cumin
1/8 teaspoon chili powder
1/8 teaspoon cayenne pepper
1/2 cup diced red bell pepper
1/4 cup diced celery
Salt and pepper to taste
2 tablespoons red wine vinegar
1/2 cup diced mango, or papaya
1/2 cup diced watermelon

Shoestring Taro

1 taro or potato, julienned
1 quart frying oil

Preparation of the Black Bean Mango Salsa

- Simmer the beans in the water about 45 minutes, until they are cooked. Add more water if necessary. Drain and reserve the beans.
- In a large sauté pan, lightly brown the onions in the olive oil. Add the cumin, chili powder, cayenne pepper, red bell pepper and celery. Cook the mixture for about 1 minute.
- Place the mixture in a medium stainless-steel bowl and season it with salt and pepper.
- Add the red wine vinegar, fruit and black beans, and mix well.

Preparation of the Shoestring Taro

- Soak the taro strips in water for 30 minutes.
- Drain and rinse the strips well, then pat them dry.
In a fryer or large saucepan, fry the strips for 1 1/2 to 2 minutes, until they are crispy and golden brown.
- Place the strips on a piece of paper towel to drain the excess oil.

Grilled Chicken

4 boneless chicken breasts
Salt and pepper to taste
2 tablespoons olive oil

Preparation of the Grilled Chicken

- Season the chicken breasts with the salt and pepper. Coat them with the olive oil and grill them for 1½ to 2 minutes per side.
- Slice the chicken at an angle.

Assembly

- Place the black bean salsa in the middle of the plate. Place the chicken slices on top of the salsa and arrange the taro over the chicken, or on the side.

DESSERT

Tropical Fruit Compote

Molokai is well known for its mangoes; in fact, it lays claim to Mapule-hu mango grove, one of the largest of its kind in Hawaii, with some 2,500 trees stretching along the island's southeastern shore. Serves 6.

Ingredients

5 tablespoons granulated sugar
1 3-inch piece ginger root, sliced ⅛ inch thick
1 cup lilikoi (passion fruit) juice, or fresh orange juice
Grated zest of 1 orange
Grated zest of 1 lemon
1 cinnamon stick
5 cloves
¼ cup chopped pineapple
1 sliced banana
1 chopped mango
¼ cup sliced kiwi fruit
¼ cup blueberries
¼ cup raspberries
1 quart vanilla ice cream

Assembly

- In a stainless-steel saucepan over moderate heat, cook the sugar, ginger and lilikoi juice about 5 to 10 minutes, until the mixture thickens.
- Add the orange and lemon zest, cinnamon, cloves and pineapple and cook the mixture for another 5 minutes over low to medium heat.
- Add the remaining fruit and cook the mixture for another 5 minutes.
- Discard the cinnamon, ginger and cloves.
- Serve warm over vanilla ice cream.

Wine Suggestion

Bonny Doon, Clos de Gilroy, Grenache, California, *or* Champalou, Vouvray, Loire Valley, France

Of Land and Sea

Roy Yamaguchi

Warm Mongolian Stirfry Beef Salad with Roasted Hawaiian Macadamia Nuts and Mint

Baked Opakapaka (Pink Snapper) in Coconut Broth

Raspberry Gratin with Passion Fruit Essence and Roasted Hawaiian Macadamia Nuts

---

SALAD

Warm Mongolian Stirfry Beef Salad with Roasted Hawaiian Macadamia Nuts and Mint

For this tangy salad, Chef Yamaguchi calls for rice wine vinegar, a light, sweet liquid made from fermented rice. It is sometimes known as Japanese rice vinegar. Serves 4.

Dressing

¼ cup rice wine vinegar, or any delicate vinegar
½ cup sugar
2 kaffir lime leaves
1 tablespoon minced cilantro
3 or 4 red Thai chilis, or jalapeño peppers
¼ cup lemon or lime juice
1 tablespoon chopped shallots
1 tablespoon minced garlic
2 tablespoons Chinese chili paste, or any garlic chili paste
1 lemongrass stalk, minced
½ cup water
1 tablespoon minced mint

Warm Mongolian Stirfry Beef Salad with Roasted Hawaiian Macadamia Nuts and Mint

Preparation of the Dressing

■ Combine all the ingredients in a medium bowl and refrigerate the mixture overnight.

Preparation of the Beef Marinade

■ Combine all the ingredients in a bowl and marinate the beef for 1 hour.

Preparation of the Vegetable Stirfry

■ In a large pan over high heat, sauté the ginger, garlic, mushrooms, radicchio, escarole, kale, onions and peppers in olive oil for about 1 minute.

■ Add the noodles and cook for 1 minute.

■ Remove the mixture from the heat and transfer it to a plate.

Beef Marinade

1/2 cup hoisin (a sweet, soy-based sauce)
2 tablespoons soy sauce
1/2 tablespoon minced ginger
1 tablespoon red wine vinegar
2 tablespoons sugar

Vegetable Stirfry

1 teaspoon minced ginger
1 teaspoon minced garlic
1/4 cup fresh shiitake mushrooms
1/2 large head radicchio, or your favorite lettuce
1 cup chopped escarole, or your favorite lettuce,
    bite-size pieces
1 cup chopped kale, or your favorite lettuce,
    bite-size pieces
1/2 Maui onion, or any sweet onion, sliced
1 red bell pepper, julienned
1 yellow bell pepper, julienned
1/4 cup olive oil
1/2 cup cooked Chinese bean thread noodles

Beef

10 ounces New York steak, cut into thin strips
2 tablespoons olive oil

Garnish

1 tablespoon roasted Hawaiian macadamia nuts

Preparation of the Beef

- Remove the beef from the marinade.
- Sauté the beef in the olive oil over extremely high heat for about 30 seconds, or until your desired doneness.

Assembly

- Place the beef over the vegetables and garnish it with the nuts.
- Sprinkle the dressing around the salad.

Baked Opakapaka in Coconut Broth

With its earthy, sometimes bitter flavor, bamboo imbues this dish with Asian overtones. It is sold in shoots that usually have been soaked in water, and it can be found either in cans or in the fresh produce section. Serves 2.

Opakapaka

1½ pound whole opakapaka (pink snapper), or any snapper, gutted and scaled

Coconut Broth

3½ cups coconut milk
½ tablespoon minced ginger
½ tablespoon minced garlic
¼ cup chopped green onion
¼ cup palm sugar (Thai sugar paste)
½ tablespoon Masaman curry (Thai curry paste), or any curry paste
3 whole basil leaves
3 lemongrass stalks, smashed with a knife

Bamboo Mixture

1 cup julienned bamboo shoots
½ cup sliced green onion, 1½-inch strips
½ cup chopped cilantro
½ cup medium-sliced fresh shiitake mushrooms

Preparation of the Opakapaka

■ Gut and scale the opakapaka and place it in a large casserole.

Preparation of the Coconut Broth

■ Combine all the ingredients in a large saucepan and simmer over medium heat for 10 minutes. Strain the liquid over the fish in the casserole.

Preparation of the Bamboo Mixture

■ Mix all the ingredients and place them over the fish.

Assembly

■ Preheat the oven to 400 degrees F.
■ Bake the casserole in the oven for 30 minutes or until the fish is cooked thoroughly.

Raspberry Gratin with Passion Fruit Essence and Roasted Hawaiian Macadamia Nuts

Better known in Hawaii as lilikoi, passion fruit grows prolifically in the islands and can be found in Asian markets on the mainland. Known for its tangy pulp, it is the edible fruit of the passion flower. Serves 6.

Crème Anglaise
8 egg yolks
½ cup granulated sugar
4 vanilla beans, split lengthwise
1 pint milk
1 pint heavy cream

Raspberry Gratin
4 cups raspberries
¼ cup Framboise liqueur
2 cups heavy cream, whipped until thickened
¼ cup lilikoi (passion fruit) syrup, or orange juice
  concentrate
½ tablespoon granulated sugar
3 tablespoons Hawaiian macadamia nuts, roasted
  and crumbled

Preparation of the Crème Anglaise
- In a medium stainless-steel bowl, whip the egg yolks with the sugar for 2 minutes until they are creamy and turn pale yellow.
- In a small saucepan, scald the vanilla beans and the milk for 2 minutes. Remove the mixture from the heat and let it sit for 1 hour.
- Combine the milk mixture with the sugar mixture and place it into a medium saucepan.
- With a wooden spoon or rubber spatula, continue to stir the mixture over low heat, always scraping the bottom and sides of the pot, for about 15 minutes or until it coats the back of the spoon.
- Add the heavy cream to the mixture and bring it back to a simmer.
- Strain the mixture, and refrigerate it for 1 hour.

Preparation of the Raspberry Gratin
- Preheat the broiler.
- Toss the berries with the liqueur and place them on a plate.
- Mix 2 cups of the crème anglaise with the whipped cream and lilikoi syrup. Pour the mixture over the berries.

Assembly

- Sprinkle the sugar over the sauce and place the plate under the broiler for 30 to 45 seconds, until the cream is browned and bubbly.
- Sprinkle the macadamia nuts over the gratin before serving.

Wine Suggestion

Gunderloch Nackenheimer Rothenberg Kabinett, Rheinhessen, Germany, *or*

Bonny Doon Pacific Rim Chenin Blanc, Santa Cruz, California

Family Business

In Hawaii, family is called ohana, a word that implies a great depth of love and aloha. Perhaps due to the isolated nature of the islands, the local ohana extends beyond blood relatives to include friends—affectionately known as aunties and uncles—who are there for each other in good times and bad.

Hawaii's close-knit social fabric has helped perpetuate the family business, allowing unique products and ohana relationships to survive through changing times. Near Pearl Harbor, for instance, a 10-acre watercress farm has been managed by three generations of the Sumida family. In Honolulu, Young's Fishmarket is run by Alan Young and his sister Barbara, whose parents opened the original store in 1950.

Family members play an equally important part in the success of many Hawaii restaurants. On Kauai, Jean-Marie Josselin's wife, Sophie, crafts the dinner plates for A Pacific Cafe. Beverly Gannon's husband, Joe, co-owns her Maui establishment, Haliimaile General Store. Roy Yamaguchi's wife, Janne, who boasts an impressive artistic background, works behind the scenes on a half-dozen projects at a time, from overseeing the interior design of each new restaurant in her husband's chain, to selecting the design of the house wine labels, choosing employees' uniforms and coordinating the restaurants' ongoing local art exhibitions.

Grilled Pork Medallions with Watercress Salad

A is for Ahi

Roy Yamaguchi

Grilled Teriyaki Ahi (Bigeye Tuna) with Niçoise Olives and Feta Cheese

Maui Onion Soup with Goat Cheese Crostini

Grilled Pork Medallions with Watercress Salad

Tropical Sorbet

APPETIZER

Grilled Teriyaki Ahi with Niçoise Olives and Feta Cheese

When served raw as Japanese sashimi, ahi (bigeye tuna) is a buttery delicacy enlivened by wasabi (Japanese horseradish) and soy sauce. It is equally delicious in the following preparation, in which the flavor of the fish is enhanced by an Asian marinade. Serves 4.

Teriyaki Sauce and Ahi

1 cup soy sauce
1 tablespoon minced garlic
1 tablespoon minced ginger
1 cup sugar
1 teaspoon white sesame seeds, roasted
14-ounce ahi (tuna) steak, or swordfish, cut into
   4 equal portions

Dressing

1 shallot, minced
1 clove garlic, minced
¼ cup olive oil
2 tablespoons sherry vinegar
Salt and pepper to taste

Preparation of the Teriyaki Sauce and Ahi

■ Combine the soy sauce, garlic, ginger, sugar and sesame seeds in a large bowl, and marinate the ahi in the mixture for 30 minutes.

■ Grill the ahi for 30 seconds to 1 minute per side, until desired doneness.

Preparation of the Dressing

■ Sauté the shallots and garlic in the olive oil in a skillet over medium heat for 10 seconds.

■ Add the vinegar, and season the mixture with the salt and pepper.

Assembly

5 cups mixed greens

16 Niçoise (small French) olives, or high-quality California green olives

4 eggs, hard-boiled and quartered

½ cup green beans, boiled until just tender and drained

4 new potatoes, boiled until tender and quartered

Garnish

2 tablespoons crumbled feta cheese

Assembly

- Divide the greens equally among 4 plates.
- Place equal amounts of the olives, eggs, beans and potatoes around the salad on each plate.
- Place the grilled ahi over the salad mixture, and pour the dressing over the ahi, beans, eggs, potatoes and olives. Garnish with the feta cheese.

SOUP

Maui Onion Soup with Goat Cheese Crostini

Similar to Vidalias or other sweet, mild varieties, Maui onions thrive in Hawaii's volcanic soil. Farmers in the upcountry regions of Maui have experienced particular success growing them. Serves 4.

Soup

2 tablespoons olive oil

2 to 3 Maui onions, or any sweet onion, sliced thin

3 cloves garlic, minced

1 quart chicken stock

Goat Cheese Crostini

8 (½-by-2½-inch) French bread slices

¼ cup goat cheese

4 sun-dried tomatoes

1 teaspoon fresh minced basil

Garnish

⅓ cup grated parmesan cheese

Preparation of the Soup

- Place the oil in a soup pot over high heat. Sauté the onions with the garlic for 2 to 3 minutes, until they are lightly browned. Add the chicken stock, turn down the flame, and simmer the soup for 30 minutes.

Preparation of the Goat Cheese Crostini

- Preheat the broiler.
- Toast the bread slices on both sides under the broiler.
- Mix the goat cheese, sun-dried tomatoes and basil in a small bowl. Spread the mixture to cover one side of each bread slice.

Assembly

- Preheat the broiler.
- Divide the soup among 4 soup bowls. Place 2 goat cheese crostini in each bowl, and cover them with equal amounts of the parmesan cheese.
- Place the bowl under the broiler. Broil for 1 minute, until the cheese is golden brown.

Grilled Pork Medallions with Watercress Salad

For crispier shoestring potatoes, first soak them in water to remove the starch. Rinse them well, and dry them thoroughly before frying.
Serves 4.

Pork
1 quart warm water
1 green bell pepper, chopped
1/2 onion, chopped
2 bay leaves
10 peppercorns
1/2 cup sugar
4 (7-ounce) pork chops, or 2 pork tenderloins

Watercress Bed
2 tablespoons sesame oil
1/2 teaspoon minced ginger
1/2 teaspoon minced garlic
2 cups fresh shiitake mushrooms, sliced
1/2 cup watercress stems
1 cup red bell peppers, sliced in thin strips
2 cups bean sprouts
1/2 tablespoon oyster sauce
1 teaspoon white sesame seeds

Shoestring Potatoes
1 potato, julienned
1 pint oil for frying

Watercress Salad
3 tablespoons olive oil
1/8 teaspoon minced ginger
1/8 teaspoon minced garlic
1/2 teaspoon chili paste
3 tablespoons rice wine vinegar, or any delicate vinegar
10 cups (1/2 pound) watercress leaves, top 2 inches
2 to 4 tablespoons roasted, crushed Hawaiian macadamia nuts

Preparation of the Pork
■ Combine all the ingredients in a large bowl and marinate the pork overnight.
■ Grill the pork to desired doneness. Slice it into 1/8-inch-thick medallions, and set it aside.

Preparation of the Watercress Bed
■ Heat the sesame oil in a medium sauté pan. Sauté the ginger, garlic, mushrooms, watercress stems and bell peppers over medium heat for 1 minute.
■ Add the bean sprouts and oyster sauce. Sauté the mixture for another 30 seconds, and sprinkle in the sesame seeds. Set the mixture aside.

Preparation of the Shoestring Potatoes
■ Soak the thin potato slivers in water for 1 hour.
■ Drain and rinse the potato well, then pat dry.
■ In a fryer or large saucepan, fry the potato in the oil for 1 1/2 to 2 minutes, until the slivers are crispy and golden brown.
■ Place the potato on a piece of paper towel to drain the excess oil.
■ Reserve a handful of shoestring pieces for garnish.

Preparation of the Watercress Salad
■ Heat the olive oil in a large pan, and sauté the ginger and garlic for 15 seconds. Add the chili paste and vinegar.
■ Remove the mixture from the heat, and place it in a large salad bowl. Add the watercress and macadamia nuts, and toss with the shoestring potatoes.

Assembly

- Divide the watercress bed equally among 4 plates.
- Place the pork on top of the bed, and place the watercress salad on top of the pork.
- Place the remaining shoestring potatoes on top of the watercress salad.

Tropical Sorbet

The sweet flavors of ripe pineapple, papaya and guava transform a standard sherbet into tropical ambrosia. Serves 8.

Ingredients

1¼ cups fresh pineapple pulp, pureed
1¼ cups fresh papaya pulp, pureed
1¼ cups fresh guava pulp, pureed
1⅛ cups granulated sugar

Assembly

- Combine the fruits with the sugar in a large bowl. Place the mixture into an ice cream maker.
- Follow the instructions provided with the ice cream maker to finish the sorbet.

Wine Suggestion

Au Bon Climat, Pinot Noir, Santa Barbara, California, *or*
Robert Sinskey, Pinot Noir, Carneros, California, *or*
Aubert de Villaine, Bourgogne "La Digoire," Burgundy, France

Kauai Ohana

Jean-Marie Josselin

Crabmeat Wonton with Ponzu Dip

Opakapaka (Pink Snapper) and Clam Chowder

Steamed Lamb Loin with Tamarind Plum Sauce

Sleeping Giant Lemon Tartlets

APPETIZER
Crabmeat Wonton with Ponzu Dip

Ponzu is a sauce derived from Japanese culinary tradition. Chef Josselin says the flavors of citrus and soy sauce in the dip provide the ideal balance to the crabmeat filling of the wonton. Makes 12 wonton.

Ponzu Dip
3 tablespoons light soy sauce
2 tablespoons mirin (sweet rice wine)
2½ tablespoons lime juice
2 tablespoons orange juice

Wonton
1 pound crabmeat, shredded
Pinch of cayenne pepper
1 egg, lightly beaten
1 tablespoon heavy cream
½ teaspoon chopped fresh cilantro
Juice of ½ lemon
2 teaspoons diced red bell pepper
12 square wonton wrappers
Oil for deep-frying

Preparation of the Ponzu Dip
■ In a small bowl, combine the soy sauce, mirin, lime juice and orange juice, and set the mixture aside.

Assembly
■ In a mixing bowl, combine the crabmeat, cayenne, egg, cream, cilantro, lemon juice and red pepper. Blend the ingredients well.
■ Place 1 teaspoon of the filling in the center of each wonton wrapper. Secure the wrappers by bringing the four corners together and pinching well to seal them, or simply fold the wrappers in half.
■ Heat the oil to 375 degrees F in a deep-fat fryer. Fry the wontons in the oil for 1 minute, until they are golden brown. Serve at once with the dip.

Sleeping Giant Lemon Tart

Opakapaka and Clam Chowder

Jean-Marie Josselin often serves this hearty, almost stewlike chowder with crispy lavosh (unleavened bread). Serves 6.

Roux
6 tablespoons (³/₄ stick) unsalted butter
¹/₄ cup all-purpose flour

Opakapaka
¹/₄ cup olive oil
10 ounces opakapaka (pink snapper), or red snapper, cut into ¹/₂-inch cubes
Salt and pepper to taste

Chowder
1 tablespoon chopped fresh ginger
2 teaspoons chopped garlic
1 medium potato, peeled and diced into ¹/₂-inch cubes
1 medium carrot, peeled and diced into ¹/₂-inch cubes
2 celery stalks, diced into ¹/₂-inch cubes
1 small onion, peeled and diced into ¹/₂-inch cubes
4 large button mushrooms
¹/₂ cup dry white wine
¹/₂ cup dry sherry
30 small clams
2 cups fish stock
2 cups clam juice
1 cup heavy cream
Salt and pepper to taste
Juice of 1 lemon

Preparation of the Roux
■ Melt the butter in a heavy pan, and stir in the flour. Cook the mixture over medium heat for 5 minutes, stirring constantly until it is a light brown paste, and set it aside.

Preparation of the Opakapaka
■ Heat the olive oil in a large nonreactive saucepan. Lightly sauté the opakapaka for 2 minutes, seasoning it with the salt and pepper. Remove the fish with a slotted spoon, and set it aside.

Preparation of the Chowder
■ In the same pan, sauté the vegetables in the remaining oil, beginning with the ginger and garlic, then adding the potato, carrot, celery, onion and mushrooms, one after the other in order. Cook each addition for 3 minutes.
■ Add the wine and sherry, and bring the mixture to a boil. Add the clams, cover the saucepan, and cook the mixture for 5 minutes.
■ Remove the clams with a slotted spoon, and scrape the clams from their shells. Place the clams on the side, and discard the shells.
■ Add the fish stock and clam juice, and bring the mixture to a boil.
■ Reduce the heat, and simmer for 5 minutes.
■ Add the roux and the cream, stirring well to avoid lumps. Cook the mixture for 10 minutes.

Assembly
■ Return the clams and the opakapaka to the chowder, season it with salt and pepper, and finish with the lemon juice.
■ Serve the chowder in warmed soup bowls.

Steamed Lamb Loin with Tamarind Plum Sauce

A standard in Asian markets, tamarind pulp comes from the pods of the tamarind tree. Its lemony flavor adds a pleasant tartness to sauces. Serves 4.

Lamb Loin
4 (8-ounce) lamb chops
Salt and freshly ground pepper to taste
Cayenne pepper to taste

Vegetable Mixture
1 large zucchini, julienned fine
2 yellow summer squash, julienned fine
4 leeks, white part only, julienned fine
4-inch piece ginger, peeled and cut into four
   (1-inch) chunks

Tamarind Plum Sauce
4 teaspoons cornstarch
1/3 cup cold water
2 cups dry red wine
4 ripe plums, pitted
2 tablespoons seedless tamarind pulp
1 quart chicken stock
Salt and pepper to taste

Wrappers
4 sheets rice paper
8 leaves bok choy

Preparation of the Lamb Loin
■ Season the lamb with the salt, pepper and cayenne. Set aside.

Preparation of the Vegetable Mixture
■ Combine all the ingredients in a medium bowl. Set aside.

Preparation of the Tamarind Plum Sauce (Makes 1½ cups)
■ Combine the cornstarch and water in a small bowl. Set aside.
■ Combine the wine, plums and tamarind in a saucepan. Bring the mixture to a boil, and reduce the heat. Cook until the mixture is reduced by ¾, to ½ cup.
■ Add the chicken stock and bring to a boil. Reduce the heat and simmer for about 5 minutes.
■ Whisk in the cornstarch mixture, and cook for another 5 minutes. Strain the sauce, and season with the salt and pepper.

Assembly
■ Moisten each sheet of the rice paper, and line it with 2 bok choy leaves. Place ¼ of the vegetable mixture on each wrapper, and add a lamb slice. Wrap the meat tightly in the bok choy leaves and rice paper.
■ Gently place the lamb packages in a bamboo steamer and cover it. Steam the packages over boiling water for 6 minutes, at which point the lamb should be medium-rare. Allow it to cool for 1 minute.
■ Cut the lamb packages into 1½-inch slices. Place ½ cup of sauce on each serving plate, and place the slices on top of the sauce (one sliced lamb package per plate). Serve any remaining sauce separately.

Sleeping Giant Lemon Tartlets

In a tribute to the dramatic geography of Kauai, Josselin has fashioned a mountainous dessert that reminds him of the Wailua rock formation called Sleeping Giant. Makes 4 tartlets or 1 large tart.

Sugar Tart Pastry

2½ cups all-purpose flour
Pinch of salt
½ cup granulated sugar
1 cup (2 sticks) unsalted butter
¼ cup ice water

Tart Filling

1⅓ cups milk
4 egg yolks
½ cup lemon juice
2 teaspoons grated lemon rind
4 teaspoons granulated sugar

Meringue

5 egg whites
1 tablespoon granulated sugar

Preparation of the Sugar Tart Pastry

■ Combine the flour, salt and sugar in a mixing bowl. Cut the butter into small pieces, and add it to the mixture, working it by hand until it is well blended.
■ Add the water little by little, working the dough by hand for 1 minute until it holds together well. It should not be wet or sticky.
■ Place the dough in a plastic bag, and refrigerate it for 1 hour.
■ Preheat the oven to 375 degrees F.
■ On a lightly floured table, roll the dough to a ⅛-inch thickness. Place it in 4 small tartlet molds or 1 (11-inch) tart mold, pinching it along the sides of the mold. Cover the pastry with aluminum foil, and weigh it down with beans or pastry weights so that it will not bubble.
■ Pre-bake the tartlets for 6 minutes. Remove them from the oven to cool, but leave the oven on.

Preparation of the Tart Filling

■ In a medium mixing bowl, combine the milk, egg yolks, lemon juice, lemon rind and sugar.
■ Pour the filling into the tartlet shells, and bake them for approximately 20 minutes, or until the filling is set. Let the tartlets cool completely.

Preparation of the Meringue
■ Whip the egg whites in a mixer or with a hand beater, until they are almost stiff. Add the sugar and beat the mixture until it is stiff.

Assembly
■ Preheat the broiler.
■ Spread the meringue into mountainlike peaks on each tartlet, and place them under the broiler for 10 to 15 seconds to caramelize the sugar and brown the meringue.

Wine Suggestion
Mas de Daumas Rouge, Languedoc, France, *or*
Shafer Merlot, Napa Valley, California

Maui

Maui is an island with multiple personalities. It offers peaceful pastures as well as noisy nightclubs, hikes from the top of a 10,023-foot dormant volcano and sea-level whale watching and scuba diving. It imparts a sense of history, as told by the weathered 19th-century buildings of Lahaina town, and it nods to the 1990s with such facilities as a 50,000-square-foot Wailea Resort spa. By day, you can sit on a beach and slurp some shave ice (a snow cone with tropical syrups), and come evening you can dine by candlelight on kiawe (mesquite)-fired baby lamb chops with fresh guava coulis and Maui onion mashed potatoes.

Beverly Gannon (Haliimaile General Store), David Abella (Roy's Kahana Bar & Grill), Roger Dikon (Maui Prince) and Mark Ellman (Avalon) are four Hawaii chefs who have chosen to ply their trade on Maui. Small wonder: Each day, pickup trucks pull up to their back doors with crates full of home-grown avocados, tomatoes, strawberries and basil. Farmers have discovered how to coax fresh, flavorful products out of the rich volcanic soil of upcountry Maui, and chefs keep the growers on speed dial to find out what's currently available. In independent restaurants as well as swank hotels, menus make the most of Maui's bounty, whether it's sweet onions from Kula, lemongrass stems from Hana, organic herbs from Paia, pineapple from Wailuku or papayas from Haiku.

Chocolate Macadamia Nut Tart

Stirfry and Such

Beverly Gannon

Sashimi Sampler

Asian Stirfry over Crispy Noodles

Grilled Ahi (Bigeye Tuna) in Tomato Beurre Blanc

Chocolate Macadamia Nut Tart

APPETIZER

Sashimi Sampler

The most common method of serving sashimi (thinly sliced raw, high-grade fish) is with a hot paste called wasabi (Japanese horseradish) mixed with soy sauce. For variety, Beverly Gannon comes up with two additional presentations. Serves 6.

Ahi
18 ounces sashimi-grade ahi (bigeye tuna), or any high-grade fish

Blackened Sashimi
1/4 cup blackening spices (from your grocer's gourmet section)
2 tablespoons oil
1/4 cup Thai chili sauce, or Chinese chili paste

Sashimi Tartare
2 tablespoons mayonnaise
1 tablespoon Thai chili sauce, or Chinese chili paste
1 tablespoon chopped scallions

Preparation of the Ahi
■ Separate the ahi into 3 (6-ounce) strips.

Preparation of the Blackened Sashimi
■ Roll one ahi strip in the blackening spices. Sear the ahi in the oil in a very hot pan, about 10 seconds per side.
■ Let the ahi cool, then slice it into 18 pieces.

Preparation of the Sashimi Tartare
■ Finely dice the second ahi strip. Combine the mayonnaise, chili sauce and scallions in a medium bowl. Add the ahi, mix all the ingredients and chill them for 30 minutes, or until serving time.

Sashimi

¼ cup soy sauce

1 teaspoon wasabi paste (Japanese horseradish)

Garnish

1½ cup mixed greens

3 teaspoons sesame seeds

Asian Pesto

1 bunch cilantro with stems

1 small piece ginger root

1 clove garlic

2 stalks lemongrass (root end)

¼ cup peanut oil

2 shallots

1 tablespoon Vietnamese red chili paste, or any oriental chili paste

Asian Spice

2 teaspoons Szechuan peppercorns

1 teaspoon whole black peppercorns

1 teaspoon whole coriander seeds

1 teaspoon whole cumin seeds

1 whole star anise

½ teaspoon garlic powder

Sauce

2 tablespoons oyster sauce

1 tablespoon fish sauce

¼ cup fish or vegetable stock

Preparation of the Sashimi

- Slice the remaining ahi strip on the bias into 18 pieces. Set aside.
- In a small bowl, combine the soy sauce and wasabi.

Assembly

- Arrange the three sashimi preparations on a large platter.
- Spoon the Thai chili sauce over the blackened sashimi.
- Serve the thinly sliced sashimi with the soy sauce/wasabi mixture.
- Garnish the platter with the mixed greens and sesame seeds.

SIDE DISH

Asian Stirfry Over Noodles

The noodles in this dish can be cooked and served al dente, or they can then be fried in a pan of smoking hot oil until they are puffed and crispy. Makes 2 hearty servings.

Preparation of the Asian Pesto

- Grind all the ingredients together in a food processor until they are well mixed, and set aside.

Preparation of the Asian Spice

- Roast all the ingredients in a dry pan over high heat, approximately 3 to 4 minutes. Remove them from the pan and grind them in a coffee grinder until they become a medium-grain powder.

Preparation of the Sauce

- Mix all the ingredients together well, and set aside.

Preparation of the Noodles

- Cook the noodles in boiling salted water for 1 minute. Drain and rinse the noodles and set them aside.
- Optional: Next, pan-fry the noodles in smoking oil for 5 to 7 minutes, stirring to avoid burning. Dry them on a paper towel.

Seafood
4 raw clams
4 raw scallops
4 raw shrimp
4 (1-ounce) pieces fresh fish of your choice

Noodles
1 (12-ounce) package soba (buckwheat) noodles,
 or angel hair pasta
Oil for pan-frying (optional)

Stirfry
2 tablespoons peanut oil
1 teaspoon sesame oil

Vegetables
1 small onion, julienned
10 sugar snap peas
1 red pepper, julienned
1 carrot, julienned
1 handful mixed greens

Ahi
2 (6-ounce) ahi (bigeye tuna) steaks, or your
 favorite fish
Salt and cracked black pepper to taste
1 teaspoon olive oil

Tomato Beurre Blanc
6 tablespoons white wine
1 clove of garlic, chopped fine
6 tablespoons heavy cream
Juice of 1 lemon
1 ripe tomato, peeled and chopped fine
1 ½ sticks (¾ cup) cold butter
1 shallot, chopped fine
1 sprig fresh thyme
1 sprig basil
3 sprigs fresh dill
Salt and pepper to taste

Assembly
- Heat the peanut and sesame oils in a very hot wok.
- Sprinkle the seafood with the Asian spice and place it in the wok. Sear the seafood so that it turns brown, approximately 3 to 4 minutes.
- Stir in 1 tablespoon of the Asian pesto. Add the vegetables and stirfry the mixture for 30 seconds.
- Add the sauce and stirfry the mixture for 1 minute.
- Place the noodles (or crispy noodles) on 2 plates and serve the stirfry on top of them.

Entree
Grilled Ahi in Tomato Beurre Blanc

Beverly Gannon likes this combination because "fish and tomatoes are a perfect marriage. In fact, fish with any kind of butter sauce tastes great." She adds that ahi should not be overcooked or it will get dry. Serves 2.

Preparation of the Tomato Beurre Blanc Sauce
- In a medium saucepan, combine the wine, garlic, cream, lemon juice and tomato.
- Reduce the mixture for 4 to 5 minutes, until it starts to thicken.
- Using a whisk, whip the butter into the mixture over low heat. Remove the pan from the stove.
- Add the herbs and seasonings and set the mixture aside.

Preparation of the Ahi
- Rub the ahi with the salt, pepper and oil. Grill the ahi on a hot grill, or broil for 1 minute on each side for rare (longer for well-done).

Garnish

Sliced starfruit, or papaya, mango or lemon

Assembly

■ Spoon the beurre blanc on 2 plates. Place the ahi on the sauce, and garnish it with the starfruit.

Chocolate Macadamia Nut Tart

The chocolate pastry shell used here is a cookie-like crust. The dough softens quickly once it is out of the refrigerator, and it is a bit difficult to transfer to the tart pan, but scraps may be used to repair any cracks. Serves 8.

Chocolate Pastry Shell

2 cups flour
1/4 cup unsweetened cocoa
1 1/2 sticks unsalted butter, cut into pieces and softened to room temperature
1/2 cup sugar
2 egg yolks
1 tablespoon heavy cream
1 teaspoon vanilla extract
1/2 teaspoon salt

Filling

1 1/2 cups unsalted Hawaiian macadamia nuts
6 ounces bittersweet chocolate, coarsely chopped
2 tablespoons unsalted butter
2 eggs
1 egg white
2/3 cup sugar
2/3 cup dark corn syrup
1 teaspoon rum

Garnish

Unsweetened whipped cream

Preparation of the Chocolate Pastry Shell

■ On a work surface, mix the flour and cocoa until they are well blended.
■ Form the mixture into a mound. Make a well in the center of the mound and add the remaining ingredients.
■ Using your hands, slowly blend the ingredients in the well until they are partially mixed, then incorporate the flour and cocoa until they are completely combined and a soft dough forms.
■ Pat the dough into a round shape, wrap it well with plastic wrap and refrigerate it for at least 2 hours or overnight.
■ Between two sheets of waxed paper, roll out dough into a 13-inch round. Refrigerate the dough for 10 minutes.
■ Remove the waxed paper and transfer the dough to an 11-inch tart pan with a removable bottom. Fit the dough evenly into the pan and trim any overhanging pastry. Refrigerate the dough for at least 10 minutes.
■ Preheat the oven to 425 degrees F.
■ Line the chilled shell with aluminum foil and weigh it down with pie weights or dried beans. Bake the shell for 10 minutes.
■ Remove the foil and weights and bake the shell for 5 minutes, until it has set but is slightly soft.

Preparation of the Filling

- Preheat the oven to 300 degrees F.
- Spread the macadamia nuts on a small baking sheet and roast them for 8 minutes, shaking and turning them once or twice, until they are fragrant and golden. Let the nuts cool, then coarsely chop them.
- Place the nuts in a medium skillet and toast them over low heat, stirring often until they turn golden brown all over, about 8 minutes. Be careful not to burn them. Set the nuts aside to cool completely.
- Increase the oven temperature to 350 degrees F.
- In a double boiler, melt the chocolate and butter while stirring over moderate heat. Set the mixture aside to cool it slightly.
- In a large bowl, whisk the eggs, egg white, sugar and corn syrup until they have combined. Stir in the rum, cooled chocolate mixture and nuts until they are blended.

Assembly

- Pour the filling into the partially baked chocolate pastry shell and bake it for 45 minutes, until the center is set and does not wiggle when shaken. Set it aside to cool on a rack.
- Serve the tart at room temperature or chilled, garnished with the whipped cream.

Wine Suggestion

Regaleali Rosato, Sicily, Italy, *or*
Babcock Chardonnay, Santa Barbara, California

Made on Maui

David Abella

━━━━━━━━━━━━━━━━━━━━━━━━━━━━━━━━━━

Crispy Asian-Style Hamachi (Yellowtail) Rolls with a Chili Lime Sauce

Kiawe-Grilled Opakapaka (Pink Snapper) Chopsticks with Shiitake Mushrooms
   and Maui Onions

Imu-Roasted Pork

Chocolate Soufflé

━━━━━━━━━━━━━━━━━━━━━━━━━━━━━━━━━━

APPETIZER
Crispy Asian-Style Hamachi Rolls with a Chili Lime Sauce

For this hamachi (yellowtail)-based dish, David Abella specifies Yamasa soy sauce because "it is less salty and more rounded than other varieties." Yamasa is available in most Asian markets and grocery stores. Serves 4.

Hamachi Mixture
2 tablespoons sesame oil
2 tablespoons olive oil
1 tablespoon minced garlic
1 tablespoon minced ginger
1/2 cup julienned carrots
1/2 cup julienned fresh shiitake mushrooms
1/2 cup bean sprouts
1/2 cup bean thread noodles
2 tablespoons Yamasa soy sauce
2 tablespoons fish sauce
1 cup chopped cilantro
1/2 cup julienned jicama (large turniplike root),
   optional

Preparation of the Hamachi Mixture
■ Combine the sesame oil, olive oil, garlic and ginger in a sauté pan over high heat. Add the carrots, shiitake mushrooms and bean sprouts, and sauté them for 30 seconds, then remove them from the heat.

■ Cook the bean thread noodles in boiling water for 3 to 4 minutes, then strain them. Add the soy sauce, fish sauce and cilantro to the bean thread noodles.

■ In a large bowl, combine the carrot/mushroom/sprout mixture, the bean thread noodle mixture, the jicama, the kaiware sprouts and the Japanese cucumber.

½ cup kaiware sprouts (Japanese radish sprouts)
½ Japanese cucumber, cut into narrow 2-inch
   sticks

Hamachi Rolls
8 rice paper wrappers
¼ pound fresh hamachi (yellowtail), or salmon,
   cut into 4 strips
1 beaten egg, for egg wash
Cornstarch for dusting
1½ cups peanut oil for frying

Chili Lime Sauce
2 cups mirin (sweet Japanese rice wine)
½ cup plum sake (available in Asian markets)
½ cup Lingham chili sauce, or any Asian chili
   sauce
3 overripe plums, seeded and diced
½ orange, squeezed
1 cup chopped cilantro
Juice of 10 limes
3 kaffir lime leaves, julienned ultra-fine

Garnish
1 bunch cilantro
2 teaspoons roasted sesame seeds

Preparation of the Hamachi Rolls
■ Soak the rice paper for 30 seconds, until it is soft. Dry it and set it aside on a dry cloth.
■ Place a strip of hamachi on the bottom of each piece of rice paper. Place ½ cup of the hamachi mixture on the paper. Brush the ends of the paper with the egg wash. Roll the paper tightly, closing the ends, and dust the roll with cornstarch.
■ In a heavy skillet, pan-fry the rolls in hot peanut oil over medium-high heat for 1 minute per side, until they are golden brown. Remove the rolls from the oil, and dab off the excess oil.

Preparation of the Chili Lime Sauce
■ Combine all the ingredients in a heavy saucepan. Bring them to a boil, and reduce the mixture for 8 to 10 minutes.
■ Remove the orange rind and combine the remaining mixture in a blender on pulse for 30 seconds.

Assembly
■ Spoon 3 tablespoons of the chili lime sauce on a warm plate. Cut the rolls in half with a serrated knife, arrange them on the plate and garnish them with the cilantro and sesame seeds.

SIDE DISH
Kiawe-Grilled Opakapaka Chopsticks with Shiitake Mushrooms and Maui Onions

Kiawe (mesquite) is a fragrant island wood often used to enrich the flavor of barbecued fish. To prepare the opakapaka (pink snapper) for this recipe, you can also cook it on a standard charcoal grill. Serves 2.

Preparation of the Vegetables
■ Pour the extra-virgin olive oil into a large heavy saucepan over medium-high heat. Add the onions and mushrooms. Sauté the mixture for 1 minute.
■ Add the minced garlic to the pan. Sauté the garlic for 30 seconds, until it is light brown.

Kiawe-Grilled Opakapaka Chopsticks with Shitake Mushrooms and Maui Onions

Vegetables

⅓ cup extra-virgin olive oil

½ cup diced Maui onion, large squares

4 large fresh shiitake mushroom caps, diced

1 tablespoon minced garlic

½ cup julienned basil

4 cups fresh spinach leaves

Salt and pepper to taste

2 tablespoons balsamic vinegar

½ cup fresh tomatoes, or ½ of an 8-ounce can of crushed tomatoes

Opakapaka

1 pound (two 8-ounce portions) opakapaka (pink snapper) fillet, or any flaky white fish

Oil to coat

Salt and pepper to taste

Garnish

2 tablespoons extra-virgin olive oil

2 tablespoons balsamic vinegar

Mirepoix

2 cups medium-diced onions

1 cup medium-diced celery

1 cup medium-diced carrots

2 tablespoons olive oil

Pork

½ cup oil for browning

5 pounds boneless pork butt, divided into 4 portions

3 whole star anise

1 tablespoon black peppercorns

1 stalk lemongrass

3 bay leaves

¼ vanilla bean, split lengthwise

1 ginger root, smashed with a mallet

■ Add the basil and spinach. Sauté the mixture for 1 minute, until the spinach leaves are wilted. Add salt and pepper to taste. Add the balsamic vinegar and the tomatoes, and set aside.

Preparation of the Opakapaka

■ Lightly oil the opakapaka and add salt and pepper to taste. Grill the fish to desired doneness.

■ Cut the opakapaka in long strips, about ½ inch wide.

Assembly

■ Divide the vegetable mixture between 2 large, warmed plates, making a mound in the middle of each plate.

■ Arrange the opakapaka on the vegetable mixture and garnish each plate with 1 tablespoon each of extra-virgin olive oil and balsamic vinegar. Sprinkle with freshly ground black pepper.

ENTREE

Imu-Roasted Pork

An imu is an underground oven used since ancient Hawaiian times to cook the pig for a traditional luau. An imu is not necessary for the following recipe; however, Abella calls it "imu-roasted" because he finishes the pork in the Roy's Kahana pizza oven, which he affectionately calls the imu. Serves 4.

Preparation of the Mirepoix

■ Sauté the onions, celery and carrots in the oil for 1 minute until lightly browned. Set aside.

Preparation of the Pork and Sauce:

■ Place the oil in a heavy stockpot and brown the pork on all sides over high heat. Remove the pork, and set it aside.

■ In the same skillet, add the mirepoix, anise, black peppercorns, lemongrass, bay leaves, vanilla bean and ginger root. Sauté the mixture for 2 minutes.

■ Add the red wine and 1 gallon of chicken stock. Stir in the cilantro and mint. Bring the mixture to a boil, then simmer it for 1½ hours.

2 cups red wine or port
1 gallon chicken stock
1½ cups rough-chopped mint
¼ pound (1 stick) unsalted butter

Applesauce
6 Granny Smith apples, peeled, cored and sliced
¼ cup mirin (sweet Japanese rice wine)
2 tablespoons rice wine vinegar, or any delicate vinegar
½ vanilla bean, split lengthwise
2 tablespoons unsweetened lilikoi (passion fruit) concentrate (optional)
2 tablespoons honey
1 whole star anise
½ ginger root

Assembly
3 cups chicken stock

■ Reduce the stock for 1 hour, to 2 cups, until it coats the back of a spoon. Strain the sauce through a fine strainer. Incorporate the butter into the sauce a little at a time.

Preparation of the Applesauce
■ Place all the ingredients in a heavy saucepan and cook for 30 minutes, until the apples have disintegrated.
■ Pour the mixture into a food processor and pulse it until it is smooth.

Assembly
■ Reheat the pork in the remaining 3 cups of chicken stock. Bring the stock to a boil and remove the pork from the stock, using a slotted spoon.
■ Center each piece of pork on a hot plate. Spoon the sauce over the pork and divide the applesauce among the 4 plates, spooning it over the pork.

DESSERT

Chocolate Soufflé

A classy, classic dessert made simple by Chef Abella. Serves 4.

Ingredients
6 ounces butter
6 ounces semisweet chocolate
1¼ cups sugar
¼ cup cornstarch
4 whole eggs
4 egg yolks

Assembly
■ Melt the butter and chocolate together over low heat. Set aside.
■ Combine the sugar and cornstarch in a medium bowl. Add the butter and chocolate mixture to the sugar and cornstarch mixture, then stir in the eggs and egg yolks. Chill the mixture overnight.
■ Preheat the oven to 350 degrees F.
■ Scoop the chilled mixture into 4 greased 1-by-2½-inch round metal molds. Bake the soufflés for 15 minutes.
■ Turn the soufflés out of the molds.

Wine Suggestion
Ca'del Solo, Il Pescatore, California, *or*
Jean Berail, Corbières Blanc, Languedoc, France

Healthy Cuisine

Fresh, home-grown foods and a perennially warm climate have helped a large percentage of Hawaii residents enjoy long and healthy lives.

Working to maintain that trend are such innovative doctors as Terry Shintani, whose progressive Waianae Diet Program demonstrates the restorative effects of local foods like the taro plant. "Taro is analogous to brown rice or pasta," says Shintani. "It's a whole food, not milled, so most of the fiber stays in. We should eat more taro and foods like it, and less animal and fried foods." With no cholesterol and barely one percent fat, taro is high in fiber, carbohydrates and potassium but low in sodium, and it has more calcium, iron, thiamine and riboflavin and fewer calories than an equal portion of rice.

Chefs around the state are doing their part to help people eat healthy foods. Easy access to Hawaii's produce and fish helps them do away with rich sauces and fattening ingredients. Instead, their recipes deliver complex flavors—not to mention therapeutic vitamins and minerals—provided by varieties of local basil, oregano, parsley, chives, lemongrass and spicy mixed greens. Today's harvest adds unparalleled freshness to today's cuisine, from a vine-ripened tomato salad with island herbs to a tropical sorbet of pineapple, papaya and guava.

Toybox Tomato Salad with Fresh Island Herbs, accompanied by Crostini with Herbed Ricotta Cheese and Sun-Dried Tomato Paste

Spa Cuisine

Kathleen Daelemans

Crostini with Herbed Ricotta Cheese and Sun-Dried Tomato Paste

Toybox Tomato Salad with Fresh Island Herbs

Cafe Kula Fried Chicken

Cafe Kula Chocolate Cake

Crostini with Herbed Ricotta Cheese and Sun-Dried Tomato Paste

Demonstrating her philosophy that "you can celebrate food and lose weight at the same time," Chef Daelemans presents a healthy version of an Italian appetizer. Serves 6.

Sun-Dried Tomato Paste
1 cup loosely packed sun-dried tomatoes
1 teaspoon chopped garlic
¼ cup olive oil
1 tablespoon chopped fresh herbs (oregano, basil, thyme, parsley or a combination)
Pinch of salt

Cheese Mixture
½ cup skim milk ricotta cheese
1 teaspoon chopped garlic
1 tablespoon loosely packed chopped fresh herbs (oregano, basil, thyme, parsley or a combination)
1 tablespoon packed grated Reggiano Parmigiano cheese, or any superior-quality parmesan cheese
Salt to taste

Preparation of the Sun-Dried Tomato Paste
■ Place the tomatoes in a bowl and cover them with very hot water for 10 minutes, until they plump up a bit. Drain the tomatoes.
■ Place all the ingredients in a food processor fitted with a sharp blade. Pulse the mixture 4 times, until it is roughly chopped, not completely smooth.

Preparation of the Cheese Mixture
■ Mix all the ingredients with a rubber spatula in a medium stainless-steel bowl, until blended.

Preparation of the Bread
■ Toast the bread slices, then rub them with the garlic clove.

Bread

6 slices whole wheat, sourdough or your favorite bread

1 clove garlic (peeled)

Toybox Tomato Salad with Fresh Island Herbs

"Toybox" refers to an assortment of colorful miniature tomatoes such as Sweet 100s, yellow pear, red pear and cherry. Kathleen Daelemans also works with large red and yellow tomatoes, green tiger stripes and golden jubilees that are brought by farmers from upcountry Kula. Serves 6.

Assembly

■ Spread equal amounts of the tomato paste on the bread slices. Top them with the cheese mixture.

Tomatoes

2 large beefsteak tomatoes

1 large ripe yellow tomato (optional)

1 pint basket toybox tomatoes

½ cup loosely packed chopped fresh herbs (basil, parsley, cilantro, chives, thyme)

2 tablespoons balsamic vinegar

Assembly

Ground black pepper to taste

¾ cup edible flowers (marigolds, chive blossoms, orchids)

½ cup parmesan cheese shards

2 tablespoons extra-virgin olive oil to drizzle (optional)

Preparation of the Tomatoes

■ Slice the large tomatoes, and arrange them in a large dish. Cut the miniature tomatoes in half, leaving the smaller ones whole, and add them to the dish.

■ Marinate the tomatoes with the fresh herbs and vinegar until ready to serve.

Assembly

■ Arrange the tomatoes on individual salad plates. Grind the pepper over the tomatoes.

■ Garnish with the flowers and parmesan. You may choose to drizzle extra-virgin olive oil over the salad just prior to serving.

Cafe Kula Fried Chicken

Be sure to pound the chicken breasts thin and fry them in a non-stick pan that requires less olive oil. Serves 4.

Ingredients

1 1/2 cups whole wheat sourdough bread crumbs

1 tablespoon loosely packed chopped fresh oregano

1 tablespoon loosely packed chopped fresh thyme

1 tablespoon grated Reggiano Parmigiano cheese, or any superior-quality parmesan cheese

Salt and freshly cracked black pepper to taste

4 (3-ounce) boneless skinless chicken breasts, trimmed of fat and pounded thin

1/2 cup whole wheat flour

3 egg whites

1 tablespoon olive oil

Assembly

■ Combine the bread crumbs, oregano, thyme, parmesan, salt and pepper. Coat the chicken evenly with the flour. Dredge the chicken in the egg whites, then in the bread crumb mixture.

■ Heat a cast iron or stainless-steel skillet until it is very hot. Add the olive oil, and sauté the chicken breasts approximately 2 to 3 minutes per side, until they are golden brown.

Cafe Kula Chocolate Cake

Chef Daelemans' style of cooking doesn't rule out desserts; it just gives them a healthy attitude. Flavorful prunes are added to the following cake as a replacement for high-fat ingredients. Serves 10 to 12.

Ingredients

1 cup chocolate liqueur

1 cup pitted prunes

1 cup sugar

1 cup skim milk

6 tablespoons canola oil

1 tablespoon white wine vinegar

1 teaspoon vanilla

1 1/4 cups flour

1/3 cup unsweetened cocoa powder

1 tablespoon ground espresso

1 teaspoon baking soda

1 pint fresh raspberries, blended into a puree and strained if desired

1/4 cup melted bittersweet chocolate

Assembly

■ Preheat the oven to 350 degrees F.

■ Heat the liqueur and prunes in a medium saucepan for 20 minutes. Set the mixture aside, and cool it to room temperature. Blend the mixture in a food processor until smooth.

■ Slowly blend in the sugar, milk, oil, vinegar and vanilla. Gradually add the flour, cocoa powder, espresso and baking soda, blending until smooth.

■ Generously coat a springform pan, or 8-by-8-inch-pan, with non-stick spray. Pour the cake batter into the pan, and bake it for 30 to 40 minutes.

■ Place the cake on a bed of the raspberry puree, and drizzle it with the chocolate.

Wine Suggestion

Mas de Daumas, Blanc, Languedoc, France

Eating Right

Roy Yamaguchi

Shrimp and Scallop Shiu Mai in a Spicy Chili Mango Sauce

Kona Crabmeat and Grapefruit Salad

Big Island Filet with Thai Coconut Curry Sauce and Asian Vegetables

Puna Goat Cheesecake with Asian Pears

APPETIZER

Shrimp and Scallop Shiu Mai in a Spicy Chili Mango Sauce

A spicy-sweet Asian sauce adds a pleasant bite to this version of dim sum. Shiu mai is traditionally made with pork or seafood wrapped in a thin pastry, then boiled or steamed. Serves 4.

Shiu Mai Filling

½ pound raw scallops, chopped into ¼-inch pieces
½ pound raw shrimp (21–25 size), chopped medium
2 tablespoons sesame oil
1 cup minced mustard cabbage
1 cup fresh shiitake mushrooms, minced
1 teaspoon minced cilantro
1 teaspoon minced ginger
1 teaspoon minced garlic
1 medium-size green onion, minced
2 tablespoons finely diced water chestnuts
1 teaspoon fish sauce

Preparation of the Shiu Mai Filling

■ Combine the scallops and shrimp in a large bowl. Set aside.
■ Heat the sesame oil in a skillet over medium-high heat. Add the cabbage, mushrooms, cilantro, ginger, garlic, green onions and water chestnuts. Sauté the mixture for 1 minute.
■ Season the mixture with the fish sauce. Let the mixture cool, then combine it with the scallops and shrimp.

Preparation of the Shiu Mai Wrappers

■ Mix the water and cornstarch in a small bowl.
■ Lay out the wonton wrappers on a work surface, and place 1½ teaspoons of filling in the center of each wrapper. Brush the edges of the wrappers with the cornstarch mixture. Gather the wrapper edges together and twist them to close.

Shiu Mai Wrappers

6 tablespoons water
2 tablespoons cornstarch
16 square wonton wrappers

Spicy Chili Mango Sauce

1 cup Lingham chili sauce, or any spicy/sweet
 sauce
½ cup sake (Japanese rice wine)
¼ cup lilikoi (passion fruit) syrup, or orange juice
 concentrate
¼ teaspoon minced ginger
¼ teaspoon minced garlic
¼ cup water
1 teaspoon minced shallots
1 ripe mango, peeled and cut into ¼-inch cubes

Garnish (optional)

2 teaspoons white sesame seeds, roasted
4 teaspoons minced chives

■ Place the shiu mai on a pan, and refrigerate them for 1 hour.

■ Place the shui mai in a large pot of boiling water. Cook the shui mai for 5 minutes, until they float to the surface, or until the shrimp mixture is thoroughly cooked.

Preparation of the Spicy Chili Mango Sauce

■ Combine all the ingredients in a saucepan, and simmer slowly for 15 minutes, until it becomes thick.

Assembly

■ Place 4 shiu mai in each bowl and pour ¼ cup of sauce over them.

■ Garnish with the sesame seeds and chives.

Shrimp and Scallop Shiu Mai in a Spicy Chili Mango Sauce, accompanied by Kona Crabmeat and Grapefruit Salad

Kona Crabmeat and Grapefruit Salad

A refreshing warm-weather salad whose sweet, rich crabmeat wakes up to tangy fresh grapefruit sections. Serves 4.

Crab Paste
2 tablespoons chopped onion
2 tablespoons chopped carrot
1½ tablespoons chopped celery
1 pound crab shells
1 tablespoon cooking oil
¼ cup chopped parsley
4 cloves garlic, minced
1 tomato, diced
2 tablespoons white wine (chardonnay or chablis)
1 quart water

Vinaigrette
1 tablespoon olive oil
1 teaspoon minced garlic
1 teaspoon minced ginger
1 teaspoon minced lemongrass
1 shallot, minced
½ tomato, diced
4 basil leaves, julienned
1 teaspoon soy sauce

Salad
1 cup asparagus tips
1 grapefruit (sections only)
5 cups baby lettuce mix
1 tablespoon minced chervil
½ pound thin young green beans, cooked
1 pound crabmeat pieces, cooked

Preparation of the Crab Paste
■ In a large saucepan, sauté the onion, carrot, celery and crab shells in the oil for 10 to 15 minutes. When the vegetables are semi-soft, stir in the parsley, garlic and tomatoes.
■ Deglaze with the wine, and reduce the mixture for 10 minutes. Add the water, cook slowly for 45 minutes, and strain.
■ Heat the strained liquid over medium heat for 2 to 5 minutes, until it is reduced to a runny paste consistency, and set aside.

Preparation of the Vinaigrette
■ Heat the oil in a medium sauté pan. Gently sauté the garlic, ginger, lemongrass and shallots for 5 to 10 seconds, until they are lightly browned.
■ Add the tomatoes. Stir the mixture for 30 seconds, and add the basil, soy sauce and 1 tablespoon of the crab paste. Remove the pan from the heat.

Assembly
■ Place the asparagus tips, grapefruit, lettuce mix and chervil in a large bowl, and toss them with the vinaigrette.
■ Divide the beans among 4 plates, and place the salad mixture over the beans.
■ Garnish with the crabmeat.

Big Island Filet with Thai Coconut Curry Sauce and Asian Vegetables

Since the days of the first paniolo (cowboys) in the 1850s, the sprawling ranchlands of the Big Island's northern district have been the source of high-quality Hawaii beef. Serves 4.

Filet

1 tablespoon minced lemongrass
1 tablespoon minced garlic
1 tablespoon minced ginger
¼ cup olive oil
1 tablespoon soy sauce
28-ounce beef loin, cut into 4 (7-ounce) filets

Thai Coconut Curry Sauce

56 ounces (7 cups) coconut milk
2 stalks lemongrass, pounded with a mallet or
    knife until smashed
½ cup palm sugar (Thai sugar paste; no
    substitute)
5 whole basil leaves
1 tablespoon fish sauce
8 cloves garlic, minced
1 2-inch piece ginger, minced
2 tablespoons Masaman curry (Thai curry paste),
    or any curry paste

Asian Vegetables

2 tablespoons sesame oil
1¼ cups choi sum (Chinese broccoli), or Napa
    cabbage
7 green beans
½ cup fresh shiitake mushrooms
1⅓ cup Chinese black fungus mushrooms,
    (reconstituted)
1 artichoke (bottom only), chopped
1 cup bean sprouts
2 small carrots, chopped
½ teaspoon minced ginger
½ teaspoon minced garlic
1 teaspoon white sesame seeds, roasted
¼ of a medium-size red bell pepper, julienned
1 teaspoon oyster sauce

Preparation of the Filet

■ In a large bowl, combine the lemongrass, garlic, ginger, olive oil and soy sauce. Marinate the filet in the bowl for 1 hour.
■ Grill the filets to desired doneness.

Preparation of the Thai Coconut Curry Sauce

■ In a large saucepan with a thick bottom, slowly simmer the coconut milk, lemongrass stalk, sugar, basil, fish sauce, garlic and ginger for 15 to 20 minutes, until the mixture has reached the consistency of half-and-half.
■ Add the curry, and cook the mixture for 5 minutes, until it coats a spoon.
■ Strain the sauce, and set aside.

Preparation of the Asian Vegetables

■ Heat the sesame oil to smoking in a large sauté pan. Add all the remaining ingredients except the oyster sauce, and sauté for 1 minute, stirring constantly.
■ Toss the mixture with the oyster sauce, and set aside.

Assembly

■ Place 1 filet on each plate. Pour ¼ cup of sauce around it, and serve it with the Asian vegetables.

Puna Goat Cheesecake with Asian Pears

Also known as the crunch pear, salad pear and by its Japanese name nashi, the Asian pear has a crisp flesh which explodes with flavor. Round rather than pear-shaped, it was first cultivated in Japan in the eighth century. Serves 6 to 8.

Cheesecake

4½ ounces Puna goat cheese, or your local goat cheese
4½ ounces cream cheese
1 cup sour cream
½ cup granulated sugar
2 tablespoons lemon juice
Zest of 1 lemon

Asian Pear Mixture

2 Asian pears, or your favorite cooking apples
¼ cup granulated sugar
¼ cup apple brandy
2 tablespoons butter

Garnish

½ cup Hawaiian macadamia nuts, roasted and crumbled

Preparation of the Cheesecake

■ Mix the goat cheese, cream cheese and sour cream in a medium bowl until creamy.

■ Using an electric mixer and a paddle, add the sugar and continue to mix for 3 minutes.

■ Add the lemon juice and zest, and mix for 3 minutes. Set aside.

Preparation of the Asian Pear Mixture

- Peel and thinly slice the pears.
- Place the sugar in a medium sauté pan over medium heat, and caramelize it slowly while stirring. After 2 to 3 minutes, the color should be an even golden brown.
- Add the pears to the sugar, and toss them for 1 minute.
- Add the brandy and dissolve the sugar again for 30 seconds to 1 minute.
- Add the butter, and incorporate it well. Remove from the heat.

Assembly

- Preheat the oven to 275 degrees F.
- Butter an 8-inch springform pan, and line the bottom of the pan with the pear mixture. Pour the cheesecake mixture over the pear mixture.
- Bake the cheesecake for 45 minutes, until it is slightly firm. Check for doneness after 30 minutes.
- Slice the cheesecake, and sprinkle it with roasted macadamia nuts.

Wine Suggestion

Milz, Reisling Spatlese, Piesporter Hofberger, Mosel, Germany

Wild Things

The end of a meal in Hawaii often means the chance to showcase the macadamia nut, one of the state's most famous ingredients. Native to Australia and first planted in Hawaii in the late 1800s, the 60-foot trees cover tens of thousands of acres on the Big Island. Chefs have come to rely on the versatile nut for more than just desserts; for instance, it is sometimes used as a breading for fried chicken or as garnish for a salad.

Island menus are further sweetened by Hawaiian Vintage Chocolate, which has worked its way into such contemporary recipes as papaya and mango with chocolate lilikoi (passion fruit) sabayon. Cultivated in the hills above Kona, the beans are stored by year, much like wine. For instance, the dry 1991 growing season produced a fruity, floral bean, while wetter 1992 resulted in a much heavier chocolate body.

Most any Hawaii dessert is well accompanied by a cup of Kona coffee, named after the southwestern district of the Big Island. Thanks to the area's porous volcanic soil, temperate climate and ample rainfall, the rich, fragrant bean has been grown there commercially since the mid-19th century. Kona coffee adds an exotic taste to familiar recipes such as burnt cream and chocolate mousse.

The simplest of all Hawaii desserts—fresh tropical fruits—grow abundantly on every island. What could be better than a cup of chopped ripe mango over vanilla ice cream, or a wedge of sweet papaya enlivened by a squeeze of tart Kau (Big Island) lime?

Mango Ice Cream Sandwich with Macadamia Nut Cookies and Tropical Fruit Compote

Mango Mania

Amy Ferguson-Ota

Ahi (Bigeye Tuna) Napoleons

Pohole (Hawaiian Fern) Salad with Waimea Tomatoes, Maui Onions and
  Sesame Dressing

Black Sesame-Cured Wild Boar Loin with Guava Sauce

Mango Ice Cream Sandwich with Macadamia Nut Cookies and
  Tropical Fruit Compote

APPETIZER
Ahi Napoleons

Lumpia are traditional Filipino appetizers similar to spring rolls. Amy Ferguson-Ota prefers to use lumpia wrappers in this recipe because of their delicacy; if wonton or egg roll wrappers are substituted, the napoleons will be slightly heavier. Serves 10.

Wasabi-Citrus Aioli
12 egg yolks
2 tablespoons finely minced garlic
2 tablespoons Dijon mustard
1/2 cup rice wine vinegar, or any delicate vinegar
1 quart olive oil
Pickled ginger to taste
Wasabi (Japanese green horseradish) powder, or
  Colman's mustard, to taste
Soy sauce, lime juice, salt and pepper to taste

Preparation of the Wasabi-Citrus Aioli
■ Mix the egg yolks, garlic, Dijon and vinegar in a blender. Slowly add the oil until blended, then fold in the ginger, wasabi and seasonings.

Preparation of the Lumpia Skins
■ Heat the oil to 350 degrees F.
■ Deep-fry the lumpia skins in the oil for 30 seconds, until they are crisp. Remove them from the oil, and dry on a paper towel.

164

Lumpia Skins

3 to 4 quarts oil for deep-frying
10 lumpia wrappers, or wonton or egg roll wrappers, each cut into 4 squares

Napoleons

30 ounces (1⅛ pounds) ahi (bigeye tuna), or any sashimi-grade fish
1 medium-sized piece daikon (Asian radish), shredded
5 medium size carrots, shredded
30 shiso (beefsteak) leaves, rolled and sliced chiffonade-style
20 stalks chives

Sesame Dressing

½ cup rice wine vinegar, or any delicate vinegar
¼ cup sesame oil
¼ cup pickled ginger
1 clove garlic, minced
Soy sauce to taste

Salad

1 pound pohole shoots, or fiddlehead ferns, cleaned
2 Waimea tomatoes, or any vine-ripened tomatoes, seeded and julienned
1 Maui onion, or any sweet onion, peeled and julienned

Garnish

1 tablespoon sesame seeds, toasted

Assembly

▪ Thinly slice the ahi on the diagonal.
▪ On each lumpia skin, place 1 slice of ahi and 1 tablespoon each of the daikon, carrots, shiso and aioli. Repeat this process to create 3 layers, until the napoleon is 3 to 4 inches high, and top it artistically with chives.

SALAD

Pohole Fern Salad with Waimea Tomatoes, Maui Onions and Sesame Dressing

Chef Ferguson-Ota buys her pohole ferns from a family in Waipio Valley on the North Shore of the Big Island. Long and slender with a succulent, almost nutty flavor, pohole are best when picked after a rain. Serves 4.

Preparation of the Sesame Dressing

▪ Mix all the ingredients together in a medium bowl.

Assembly

▪ Combine the ferns, tomatoes and onions in a large bowl. Toss them with the dressing, and garnish with the sesame seeds.

Black Sesame-Cured Wild Boar Loin with Guava Sauce

Amy Ferguson-Ota came up with this recipe after her husband took up boar hunting. While pork loin may be substituted, she says it is not quite as rich as boar. Serves 6.

Wild Boar
1/2 cup sugar
1/4 cup kosher salt
1/3 cup minced shallots
2 tablespoons minced garlic
2 tablespoons fresh thyme
2 tablespoons chopped fresh cilantro
2 tablespoons chopped lemongrass
2 tablespoons minced ginger
1 (3-pound) center cut wild boar loin, or pork loin
1/4 cup sesame oil
1 cup black sesame seeds

Guava Sauce
1 guava, peeled and seeded
1 tablespoon minced shallots
1/4 teaspoon minced garlic
1 teaspoon grated ginger root
1 tablespoon fresh lime juice
1 tablespoon rice wine vinegar, or any delicate vinegar
1 tablespoon sugar
1/4 cup salad oil
Salt to taste
1 teaspoon fresh lemon thyme leaves

Garnish
1 cup sprigs of sunflower sprouts

Preparation of the Boar

■ Combine the sugar, salt, shallots, garlic, thyme, cilantro, lemongrass and ginger in a medium bowl. Coat the boar loin with the sesame oil, and rub it throughly with the spice-herb mixture.

■ Completely coat the seasoned loin with the sesame seeds, pressing them into the meat so they will stick.

■ Wrap the loin in plastic wrap, and let it cure overnight.

■ Unwrap the boar, and place it in a smoker on an open rack. Using wood of your choice, heat the smoker to 150 degrees F. Watch the boar closely for the first 20 minutes, so that no flames ignite.

■ After 30 minutes, cool the smoker to 130 degrees F by spraying the coals with water. If you have a thermostat on your electric smoker, set it a little below 130 degrees to cool; you may still need to spray it with water.

■ Smoke the boar for 1 hour, taking caring not to overcook it. If the loins are large and still need additional cooking, but not more smoking, finish them in a 350 degree F oven, until desired doneness.

Preparation of the Guava Sauce

■ In a blender, puree the guava with the shallots, garlic and ginger. Add the lime juice, vinegar and sugar.

■ Slowly blend in the oil. Adjust the seasonings, and sprinkle in the lemon thyme.

Assembly

■ Slice the smoked boar into medallions. Ladle 1/4 cup of the guava sauce in the middle of each plate, and arrange 3 medallions on top of the sauce, fanned out from the center of the plate. Garnish the dish with a sprig of sunflower sprouts.

Mango Ice Cream Sandwich with Macadamia Nut Cookies and Tropical Fruit Compote

A glorified ice cream sandwich, this recipe takes advantage of the abundance of mangoes in Hawaii, although it works equally well when made with strawberries, blueberries or guava. Serves 6.

Cookie Dough

1 pound unsalted butter
1²/₃ cups granulated sugar
2 eggs
¼ teaspoon vanilla extract
3¹/₃ cups all-purpose flour
⅛ teaspoon salt
½ cup Hawaiian macadamia nuts, chopped

Mango Ice Cream

¾ cup half-and-half
²/₃ cup granulated sugar
3 yolks
1 cup heavy cream
¾ cup puree of mango, or strawberries,
   blueberries or guava

Tropical Fruit Compote

1 ripe mango
4 kiwi fruit
¼ fresh pineapple, or 1 cup chunked pineapple
Sugar or honey to taste

Garnish

Sprigs of mint
Tropical flowers

Preparation of the Cookie Dough

■ Preheat the oven to 350 degrees F.
■ In a medium bowl, cream the butter and sugar for 3 to 4 minutes, until the mixture is light and fluffy.
■ Beat in the eggs and vanilla. Fold in the flour, salt and nuts, and mix for 2 minutes, until a smooth dough forms.
■ Roll the cookie dough ⅛ inch thick, cut into rounds and bake them on an ungreased, lined sheet pan for 10 to 15 minutes, or until they are lightly browned around the edges.

Preparation of the Mango Ice Cream

■ Bring the half-and-half and sugar to a boil in a medium saucepan. Slowly pour the hot mixture into the egg yolks in a stainless-steel double boiler. Cook the mixture slowly, stirring continuously for 2 to 3 minutes in order to form a custard.
■ Cool the custard. Stir in the heavy cream and the mango puree, and freeze the mixture according to the directions for your ice cream machine.

Preparation of the Tropical Fruit Compote

■ Cut the fruits in consistent sizes. Mix them together in a medium bowl, and sweeten to taste with the sugar or honey.

Assembly

■ Sandwich a 1/2-cup scoop of the ice cream between two cookies, and flatten the ice cream slightly.
■ Ladle a pool of the mango puree on the center of each plate. Cut the ice cream cookie sandwiches in half and place them split-open on the plate.
■ Spoon the tropical fruit compote over the apex of the sandwich, so that it spills onto the plate and the pool of mango puree.
■ Garnish each dish with a fresh sprig of mint and a tropical flower.

Wine Suggestion

Williams & Selyem "Allen" Pinot Noir, Russian River Valley, California, *or*

Gigondas, "Domaine du Cayron," Michel Faraud, Rhone Valley, France

Happy Endings

Roy Yamaguchi

Asian-Style Lobster Spring Rolls with Black Bean Relish

Spicy Calamari Salad with Kaffir Soy Vinaigrette

Lemongrass-Crusted Shutome (Swordfish) with an Asian Hash in Beet Sauce

Chocolate Kona Coffee Mousse

APPETIZER

Asian-Style Lobster Spring Rolls with Black Bean Relish

To make the spring rolls, fold up the lumpia strips as if you were folding a flag. Makes 15 spring rolls.

Lobster Mix
1 (2¼ pound) lobster, shelled, with body, tail and
   arms separated
2 tablespoons cooking oil

Fungus Mushroom Mix
1⅓ cup dried fungus mushrooms
1½ quarts water
½ teaspoon minced ginger
½ teaspoon minced garlic
1 tablespoon cooking oil
Salt and pepper to taste

Preparation of the Lobster Mix
■ Sauté the lobster tail meat, body and arms separately in the oil over medium heat for approximately 4 minutes each, until medium in doneness. Remove the lobster from the sauté pan, and cut it into ¼-inch-thick medallions. Set aside.

Preparation of the Fungus Mushroom Mix
■ Place the fungus mushrooms in a small saucepan with the water, and boil them for 10 minutes, or until the fungus is cooked but a little firm to the bite. Drain the liquid.
■ In a hot skillet, sauté the fungus, ginger and garlic in the oil for 1 minute. Season the mixture with the salt and pepper, and set aside.

Preparation of Shiitake Mushroom Mix
■ In a large pan over medium-high heat, sauté the mushrooms, ginger, garlic and lemongrass in the oil for 30 seconds. Add the bean sprouts, season with the salt and pepper, and cook the

Shiitake Mushroom Mix
2 cups fresh shiitake mushrooms, thinly sliced
1 teaspoon minced ginger
1 teaspoon minced garlic
1 teaspoon minced lemongrass
2 tablespoons cooking oil
1 cup bean sprouts
Salt and pepper to taste

Wrapping
5 (8-inch) lumpia wrappers, each wrapper cut
    into 3 equal strips
2 small carrots, cut into 15 matchstick-size slices
1/2 avocado, cut into 15 (2-inch-long) slices
15 whole shiso (beefsteak) leaves, or mint leaves
2 teaspoons oil for frying

Black Beans
1/2 cup black beans
1 quart chicken stock

Relish
1/2 small onion, diced
1/4 cup olive oil
1 medium-size red bell pepper, diced
1/8 teaspoon cumin
1/8 teaspoon chili powder
1/8 teaspoon dry red pepper flakes
1/2 cup diced papaya
1 cup whole basil leaves
1/4 cup red wine vinegar
Salt and pepper to taste
2 tablespoons olive oil

mixture for 30 seconds. Remove the mixture from the pan, and set aside.

Assembly
■ Place the 15 lumpia strips vertical to you on a work surface. Place 1 teaspoon of the shiitake mushroom mixture 1½ inches from the bottom of each lumpia strip.
■ For each strip, place 1 carrot strip, 1 avocado strip, 1 shiso leaf and 1 tablespoon each of the lobster mix and fungus mix over the shiitake mixture.
■ Grasp the bottom left corner of the strip, and fold it over the mixture to form a triangle. Fold forward and straight up to form another triangle. Grab the right corner, and fold it to the left to form another triangle.
■ Continue the folding process until the edges are completely sealed. Cut off the remaining portion of the lumpia strip about 1 inch above the triangle, and tuck the flap into the opening to seal.
■ Pan-fry the lumpia in the oil for 30 seconds on each side, until they turn crispy. Serve the lumpia with black bean relish (see recipe below).

RELISH
Black Bean Relish

A hot and hearty accompaniment to lumpia and other pupu (hors d'oeuvres). Makes 1 cup.

Preparation of the Black Beans
■ Simmer the black beans in the chicken stock in a medium pot over medium heat for 30 minutes, or until the beans are cooked. Drain the beans, and set them aside.

Assembly
■ Brown the onions in the oil in a small pan for 2 minutes. Add the red bell pepper, and sauté the mixture for 1 minute.
■ Add the cumin, chili powder and pepper flakes, and mix well. Sauté the mixture for 30 seconds.

- Place the mixture in a medium stainless-steel bowl. Add the papaya, basil, vinegar and cooked beans. Season the mixture with salt and pepper.
- Add the olive oil, and let the bean mixture sit at room temperature for 30 minutes before serving.

SALAD

Spicy Calamari Salad with Kaffir Vinaigrette

Chef Yamaguchi has concocted a tangy Thai vinaigrette to enliven the mellow taste of the calamari. Serves 4.

Calamari
¾ pound calamari meat, or shrimp, cut in 2-inch pieces
Salt and pepper to season
2 tablespoons olive oil

Salad
½ cup bean sprouts
¼ cup Maui onion, or any sweet onion, sliced into ¾-inch length
¼ cup whole cilantro leaves
¼ cup whole basil leaves
1 tablespoon crushed Hawaiian macadamia nuts

Vinaigrette
¼ cup olive oil
¼ teaspoon minced ginger
1 teaspoon minced garlic
½ teaspoon kaffir (Asian) lime leaves
½ teaspoon lemongrass
¼ teaspoon minced shallots
¼ teaspoon sugar
½ teaspoon lemon juice
1 tablespoon fish sauce
½ tablespoon Lingham chili sauce, or any spicy/sweet sauce

Preparation of the Calamari
- Season the calamari with the salt and pepper.
- Heat the olive oil in a medium pan. Sauté the calamari over extremely high heat for 30 seconds.
- Remove the calamari from the pan, and set aside.

Preparation of the Salad
- Combine all the ingredients in a large bowl. Add the calamari, and mix well.

Preparation of the Vinaigrette
- Heat the olive oil in a medium pan. Sauté the ginger, garlic, kaffir leaves, lemongrass and shallots for 30 seconds.
- Add the sugar, lemon juice, fish sauce and chili sauce. Mix the dressing well.

Assembly
- Pour the dressing over the lettuce/calamari mixture, and divide it equally among 4 plates.

Lemongrass-Crusted Shutome with an Asian Hash in Beet Sauce

This layered entree presents a variety of fresh, crunchy ingredients balanced by a rich red sauce. Serves 4.

Shutome

2 tablespoons minced lemongrass
1 tablespoon minced garlic
1 tablespoon minced shallots
1 tablespoon minced ginger
1 teaspoon hichimi (Japanese spice blend)
1 pound shutome (swordfish), cut into 2-by 2½-inch blocks
2 tablespoons cooking oil

Asian Hash

2 tablespoons butter
¼ cup milk
1 small celery root
I small russet potato
½ cup Napa cabbage
2 medium slices ginger
1 quart water
Salt and pepper to taste

Cabernet Sauce

1 medium onion, chopped
1 carrot, chopped
1 stalk celery, chopped
4 bay leaves
5 black peppercorns
8 cloves garlic
¼ cup cooking oil
¼ cup sugar
4 cups cabernet sauvignon
1 quart veal stock

Preparation of the Shutome

■ Preheat the oven to 350 degrees F.

■ Combine the lemongrass, garlic, shallots, ginger and hichimi in a small bowl. Coat the entire shutome with the spice mixture.

■ Lightly sauté all sides of the shutome in the oil for 10 seconds on each side.

■ Roast the shutome in the oven, turning it every 1½ minutes, until it has reached medium to medium-rare doneness.

Preparation of the Asian Hash

■ Leave the oven at 350 degrees F.

■ In a small pot, melt the butter and milk together, and set aside.

■ Boil the celery root, potato, cabbage and ginger in the water for 10 minutes, until they are fully cooked. Discard the water.

■ Place the potato mixture on a sheet pan, and bake it for 5 minutes to evaporate any excess moisture.

■ Put the mixture through a small-hole meat grinder twice, and place it in a large bowl. Whip the milk and butter mixture into the celery root/potato mixture.

■ Season the hash with the salt and pepper, and set aside.

Preparation of the Cabernet Sauce

■ In a saucepan, slowly sauté the onions, carrots, celery, bay leaves, peppercorns and garlic in the oil for 5 minutes over medium heat, or until the vegetables are golden brown.

■ Add the sugar, and caramelize the mixture for 2 minutes while stirring.

■ Add the red wine, and reduce the mixture by ⅔, to 2 cups, approximately 15 to 20 minutes.

■ Add the veal stock, and simmer the mixture for 15 to 20 minutes, then strain.

Beet Sauce
1 beet, cut into cubes
1 quart water

Garnish
½ Japanese cucumber, julienned
8 wonton skins, julienned and deep-fried
½ cup Japanese spice sprouts
¼ yellow bell pepper, julienned
¼ red bell pepper, julienned

- Simmer the mixture for about 5 minutes, or until it coats the back of a spoon.

Preparation of the Beet Sauce
- Boil the beets in the water in a medium saucepan over medium heat for 10 minutes, until they are soft. Add more water if necessary.
- Remove the beets from the liquid, and set aside.
- Reduce the beet liquid for 15 to 20 minutes, to about 1 tablespoon.
- Puree the beets, and add them to 1 cup of the cabernet sauce. Bring the mixture to a boil, then strain it.
- For more beet flavor, add the 1 tablespoon of beet liquid.

Assembly
- Place the hash on a plate, and arrange the fish on top of it. Ladle ½ cup sauce to surround the fish and hash.
- Garnish with the cucumber, wonton, spice sprouts and peppers.

DESSERT

Chocolate Kona Coffee Mousse

With Hawaiian Vintage Chocolate and Kona coffee as its two main flavor sources, this is a fine example of a new Hawaii dessert. Serves 8.

Mousse
1¼ pounds semisweet Hawaiian Vintage
  Chocolate, or any high-quality chocolate
8 egg yolks
¼ cup sugar
5 cups whipping cream
¼ cup ground Kona coffee

Topping
Whipped cream
Finely ground Kona coffee

Assembly
- Break the chocolate into chunks. Place it in a stainless-steel double boiler over hot (not boiling) water for 10 minutes, until it has melted. Remove it from the heat.
- Place the egg yolks in a stainless-steel double boiler over medium-low heat. Whip the yolks for 1 minute, or until they are pale in color and hot to the touch. Add the sugar, and whip the mixture for 1 minute, until all the sugar is incorporated. Set aside.

- In a separate bowl, whip the cream for 2 to 3 minutes, until it is stiff. Add 1 cup of the whipped cream to the yolks, and mix by hand. Fold in the chocolate, and mix until smooth.
- Add the remaining whipped cream and coffee, and mix until they are incorporated.
- Using a pastry bag, pipe the mixture into wine glasses, and chill for 3 hours.
- Garnish the mousse with whipped cream and ground coffee.

Wine Suggestion
Savènnieres, Chateau d'Epiré, Loire Valley, France, *or*
"Olivet Lane" Pinot Noir, Russian River Valley, California

Chocolate Kona Coffee Mousse

Ingredients

Most of the produce, spices, sauces and noodles listed here are available at Asian or other ethnic markets; some may also be found at well-stocked grocery stores.

Ahi Bigeye or yellowfin tuna caught in the waters surrounding Hawaii; often served as sashimi. Substitute any high-grade fresh tuna.

Asian Pears Round fruit with a crisp, flavorful flesh; also known as crunch pears or nashi. Substitute your favorite cooking apples.

Bamboo Shoots Cream-colored, cone-shaped young shoots, sold fresh and in cans.

Bean Thread Noodles Fine vegetable-based pasta, also called glass or cellophane noodles, transparent when rehydrated.

Black Fungus Mushrooms Delicate Chinese mushrooms that add a crunchy texture to dishes; sold dry.

Black Trumpet Mushrooms A variety of wild, exotic mushrooms with an earthy flavor; sold dry.

Bok Choy Chinese cabbage with dark green leaves and a long white stem. Substitute Napa cabbage.

Chanterelle Mushrooms Earthy-flavored wild mushrooms cultivated by specialty farms. Substitute any exotic mushroom.

Chili Paste Thick red sauce made of chilis, onions, sugar and tamarind; used to enhance Chinese, Thai and Vietnamese recipes.

Chili Plum Sauce Sweet-and-sour Chinese sauce available in bottles and cans.

Chinese Peas Crisp, edible pods also known as snow peas or sugar peas.

Choi Sum Chinese broccoli; more slender than regular broccoli. Substitute Napa cabbage or broccoli cut into long, thin pieces.

Coconut Fruit of the coconut palm; its white meat is most often grated or flaked before use.

Coconut Milk Rich liquid made from grating fresh coconut meat, combining it with hot water and squeezing it through a filter.

Couscous Semolina, a grain commonly steamed and served with meat or vegetables in Middle Eastern dishes.

Crab Paste Thick reduction of onions, celery, carrots, garlic, tomatoes and crab shells; sold in jars.

Daikon Long Asian radish with a crisp, juicy white flesh; often used in Japanese cooking.

Fish Roe See Tobiko.

Fish Sauce A thin, strong-scented salty brown sauce made from salted fish or shrimp; a staple of Asian sauces and soups.

Galangha Thai ginger, with a lighter flesh and milder flavor than regular ginger. Substitute regular ginger.

Ginger Root Fibrous, peppery root, peeled before use, then sliced, minced, chopped or grated.

Glass Noodles See Bean Thread Noodles.

Guava Round, yellow, plum-sized tropical fruit used in juices, jams, jellies, sauces and syrups.

Gyoza See Pot Sticker Wrappers.

Hamachi Yellowtail; sometimes called rainbow runner or Hawaiian salmon. Substitute Pacific salmon.

Hawaiian Chili Peppers Small, spicy, red-orange chilis used as a lively seasoning. For 1 pepper, substitute 1 tablespoon chili pepper paste.

Hawaiian Macadamia Nuts Hard-shelled nuts with rich, buttery meat; first planted in Hawaii in 1892 and now grown and processed extensively on the Big Island and Maui. Sold in whole nuts, pieces and bits.

Hawaiian Salt Coarse white or red crystals harvested primarily on Kauai for centuries. Substitute sea salt or kosher salt.

Hawaiian Vintage Chocolate High-quality chocolate made from beans grown on the hills above Kona, on the Big Island. Substitute any superior chocolate.

Hichimi One of many types of Japanese spice blends (see Shichimi). Substitute cayenne.

Hoisin Sauce Sweet, fermented Chinese bean sauce made from soybeans, rice, garlic, chili pepper, salt and sugar.

Japanese Eggplant Long, purple-skinned vegetable with white flesh; often used in stirfry dishes.

Japanese Plum Tart, salt-pickled plum used in dressings and sauces, sometimes served as a condiment with rice; also known as ume.

Japanese Spice Sprouts See Kaiware Sprouts.

Jicama Large, bulbous turniplike root, used raw as well as cooked.

Kaffir Lime Leaves Leaves from the kaffir lime tree, often used in soups, sauces and stirfry dishes. Substitute grated lime zest.

Kahuku Shrimp Sweet shrimp cultivated in the aquaculture ponds of Kahuku, on Oahu's North Shore. Substitute red shrimp.

Kaiware Sprouts Japanese radish sprouts with a sharp, spicy flavor.

Kau Oranges Juicy citrus fruit grown in the dry, hot Kau district of the Big Island. Substitute Valencia oranges.

Keahole Shrimp Sweet shrimp aquaculturally grown on the Big Island. Substitute any sweet shrimp.

Kiawe Fragrant wood from the mesquite tree, which grows abundantly in Hawaii; usually used to grill foods.

Kiawe Honey Made from the honey of bees attracted to kiawe flowers. Substitute any clover honey.

Kona Coffee Rich coffee made from the beans that grow in southwestern regions of the Big Island. Substitute any high-quality, dark-roasted coffee.

Kona Oysters Oysters cultivated in the aquaculture farms of Keahole-Kona, on the west coast of the Big Island. Substitute Pacific oysters.

Lanchi Chili Sauce Hot garlic chili sauce from Taiwan. Subsitute any garlic chili sauce.

Lemongrass Fragrant stalk also known as citronella, frequently called for in Thai cooking; use the lower part of the stalk. Substitute lemon zest.

Lilikoi Plum-sized citrus-flavored fruit, also known as passion fruit; sometimes sold as a frozen concentrate or syrup.

Lingham Chili Sauce Sweet Malaysian sauce of chilis, onions, sugar and spices. Substitute any spicy/sweet sauce.

Lumpia Skins/Lumpia Wrappers Rectangular, thin pastry made from flour and water, used to wrap fillings for Filipino spring rolls.

Mahimahi Dolphinfish, not related to the marine mammal. Substitute any fish with firm white flesh.

Mango Fruit consisting of fragrant high-fiber pulp surrounded by a skin that turns yellow-red when ripe.

Masaman Curry Mild Thai curry paste made from a blend of dried red chilis, onions, coriander and other spices. Substitute any curry paste.

Maui Onions Sweet onions grown in the upcountry region of Maui. Substitute Vidalias or other sweet onions.

Mirin Sweet, syrupy Japanese rice wine used in sauces and marinades. Substitute 1 teaspoon of sugar for 1 tablespoon of mirin.

Moana Hawaiian name for goatfish, a mottled red bottom fish with firm, sweet white flesh. Substitute catfish.

Mochi Rice Slightly sweet glutinous rice, popular in Asian desserts; also known as sticky rice.

Mung Beans Crunchy yellow beans with green skin; a chief source of bean sprouts.

Mustard Cabbage Chinese cabbage (see Won Bok). Substitute Napa cabbage.

Nori Dried, thin sheets of black-green seaweed, widely used in Japanese cooking; usually available in packages of 10.

Ogo Hawaiian seaweed.

Ohelo Berries Small red or yellow berries, sometimes compared to the cranberry; considered sacred to the volcano goddess Pele.

Opakapaka Hawaiian pink snapper. Substitute any flaky white fish.

Opihi Quarter-sized limpets that cling to rocks along Hawaii's coastlines. Substitute small clams or mussels.

Oyster Sauce Concentrated brown sauce made from oyster juice and salt; often used in Thai and Chinese recipes.

Palm Sugar Coarse, raw, honey-colored sugar made from palm sap and used in Thai recipes. Substitute dark brown sugar.

Panko Crispy Japanese shaved bread crumbs, coarser in texture than regular bread crumbs. Substitute unseasoned fresh bread crumbs.

Papaya Yellow-skinned tropical fruit shaped like an elongated melon, with sweet salmon-colored flesh surrounding small black seeds.

Pickled Ginger Tender, pink slices of ginger root that have been pickled in rice vinegar; often used as a garnish with Japanese foods.

Poha Hawaiian name for the cape gooseberry; often used in jams, jellies, syrups and sauces.

Pohole Ferns Delicate Hawaiian ferns with a succulent, nutty flavor. Substitute fiddlehead ferns.

Portuguese Sausage Pork sausage heavily spiced with red pepper. Substitute hot Italian or Mexican sausage.

Pot Sticker Wrappers Thin, round pastry dough made from flour and water, used to wrap some kinds of Chinese dim sum; also known as gyoza.

Puna Goat Cheese Rich, creamy cheese made from the milk of goats raised in the eastern Big Island region of Puna. Substitute your local goat cheese.

Ramen Noodles One of the main varieties of Asian wheat noodles; available fresh and dried.

Red Bananas A high-fiber baking fruit that is meatier and stronger in flavor than the yellow banana. Substitute small, tart apple bananas.

Rice Paper Thin 8-inch discs made of rice flour and water, usually softened in water before wrapping foods.

Rice Wine Vinegar Light vinegar made from fermented rice. Substitute any delicate vinegar.

Sake Clear, fragrant Japanese rice wine used in cooking and as a beverage to accompany meals. Substitute dry sherry.

Shichimi Japanese spice blend including crushed red bell pepper, sesame seeds, orange peel, seaweed and poppy seeds.

Shiitake Mushrooms Brown Japanese mushrooms with meaty caps and woody stems; available both fresh and dried. Also called golden oak mushrooms.

Shiso Leaf Aromatic heart-shaped leaves of green and red. Substitute fresh basil or mint leaves. Also called beefsteak leaf.

Shutome Swordfish caught off Hawaii's shores; also known by its Hawaiian name, au.

Soba Noodles Slender Japanese buckwheat noodles with a gray-brown hue.

Soy Sauce Known in Hawaii as shoyu, a salty brown liquid made of soybeans, flour, salt and water.

Star Anise Licorice-flavored seed pod shaped like an 8-point star.

Starfruit Waxy, light-green fruit that can be cut into star-shaped slices; also called carambola.

Szechuan Peppercorns Pungent, reddish-brown Chinese spice, larger than black and white peppercorns, but not related to them.

Tamarind Sweet/sour fruit from the brown, bean-shaped pod of the tamarind tree; available in pods, powder and pulp.

Taro A nutritious tuber used since ancient Hawaiian days to make poi, a starchy edible paste; the leaves are used to wrap foods for cooking. Substitute potatoes for the root, spinach for the leaves.

Thai Basil A slightly spicy, green and red variety of basil; substitute fresh sweet basil.

Tobiko Flying fish roe; crunchy orange eggs with a sweet, fishy flavor, often used as a garnish.

Toybox Tomatoes An assortment of colorful miniature tomatoes such as Sweet 100s, yellow pear, red pear and cherry.

Wasabi Hot, green Japanese horseradish powder; when mixed with water, it creates a paste that usually accompanies Japanese sashimi. Do not substitute regular horseradish.

Won Bok Pale-green celery cabbage with a mild flavor, sometimes called Napa or Chinese cabbage.

Wonton Wrappers Very thin, square sheets of noodle dough used to wrap foods that are deep-fried, steamed or boiled in soups.

Mail Order Sources

Aloha Shoyu Co.
96-1205 Wai Hona St.
Pearl City, HI 96782

Specialty cooking sauces

Aquaculture Development Program
Department of Land
  and Natural Resources
335 Merchant Street, Rm 348
Honolulu, HI 96813

Hawaiian seaweed, ogo

Hana Herbs
P.O. Box 323
Hana, HI 96713

Fern shoots, lemongrass, basil

Hawaiian Exotic Fruit Co.
P.O. Box 1729
Pahoa, HI 96778

Organic tropical produce

Hawaiian Fruit Specialties, Ltd.
Box 701
Kilauea, HI 96754

Jams, jellies and syrups

Javellana Farm
5473 Kawaihau Rd.
Kapaa, HI 96746

Taro products

Mauna Loa Macadamia Nuts
HC01 Box 3
Hilo, HI 96720

Macadamia nut products and Kona coffee

Molokai Seafarms
P.O. Box 560
Kaunakakai, HI 96748

Marine shrimp

Acknowledgments

Hawaii businesses eagerly contributed to the production of *Pacific Bounty*. The following companies' generosity helped enrich this book:

Paradizzio, Honolulu (808-737-6300), provided the tableware pictured on pages 29, 36, 41 (napkin), 47, 72, 77, 82, 89, 95, 111 (plate), 120 (napkin), 127, 139, 146, 151, 156.

Exquisite Collection, Honolulu (808-923-0479) provided the plates and utensils pictured on pages 53, 65, 101, 115, 120, 163, 175 (plate).

Cypress, Honolulu (808-988-5373) provided the tableware pictured on pages 58, 111 (bowl), 132, 151, 175 (glass).

Hawaii Cooks with Roy Yamaguchi gratefully acknowledges the support of its underwriters. Major funding provided by Mauna Loa Macadamia Nut Corporation.

With additional funding provided by:

In-kind contributions provided by:

Air transportation provided by Aloha Airlines.

Ground transportation provided by Alamo Rent A Car.

Index

Mauna Loa
All the goodness of Hawaii

Mauna Loa Macadamia Nut Corporation is the world's premier grower, producer and marketer of macadamia nuts and other Hawaiian foods, such as Royal Kona Coffee, Punalu'u Sweetbread and Kukui Jams and Jellies.

Mauna Loa is a subsidiary of C. Brewer and Company, a diversified agribusiness in the state of Hawaii. For over 168 years, C. Brewer has grown with the Hawaiian islands and is intrinsically tied to her history.

As a leader in the development of diversified agriculture, Mauna Loa and C. Brewer are proud to support programming that brings food products from Hawaii to the kitchens of the world's greatest chefs and to promote a better understanding of Hawaii and its people.

Mauna Loa.
A Commitment to Quality

Mauna Loa produces its own line of chocolate-covered macadamia nuts.

Mauna Loa products come with a commitment to quality.

Mauna Loa farms 10,000 acres of macadamia nut trees in Hawaii.

Our orchards are located on the slopes of the Mauna Loa volcano on the Big Island of Hawaii and on the island of Maui. Our first macadamia nut trees were planted in 1946. Today, over a million trees are farmed. The trees grow to 40 feet in height and begin bearing fruit five years after planting.

The Mauna Loa processing plant in Keaau, Hawaii produces a variety of fine macadamia nut products. At the plant, each nut is carefully husked and dried. To ensure a premium quality product, the nuts are sized, sorted and inspected before roasting—since roasting masks imperfections. After roasting, the nuts are inspected again in a quality control process based on color. Only the nuts that pass this final inspection are packaged into a variety of Mauna Loa products.

For decades we've been the pioneer in producing premium macadamia nuts. Our commitment to quality is especially important because we are not just representing a company—we are representing Hawaii to the world.

For more information about Mauna Loa products, or to receive a gift catalog, call 1-800-669-5633 or write to:

Mauna Loa
H.C. 01 Box 3, Dept. HC 94
Hilo, HI 96720-9601